A Garland Series

ROMANTIC CONTEXT: POETRY

Significant Minor Poetry
1789-1830

Printed in photo-facsimile
in 128 volumes

selected and arranged by
Donald H. Reiman
The Carl H. Pforzheimer Library

Charlotte Dacre

Hours of Solitude

Two volumes in one

with an introduction
for the Garland edition by
Donald H. Reiman

Garland Publishing, Inc., New York & London

1978

Bibliographical note:

this facsimile has been made from copies
in the British Library
(11645.bb.5)

The volumes in this series have been printed on
acid-free, 250-year-life paper.

Library of Congress Cataloging in Publication Data

Dacre, Charlotte, b. 1782.
    Hours of solitude.

    (Romantic context : Poetry)
    Reprint of the 1805 ed. printed by D. N. Shury
for Hughes, London.
    I. Title. II. Series.
PR4525.D119H6   1978   821'.7   75-31190
ISBN 0-8240-2141-X

Printed in the United States of America

Introduction

Charlotte Dacre was born about 1783, the date deduced from her declaration in the notice "To the Public" in *Hours of Solitude* (which appeared early in 1806) that she had reached "the age of three-and-twenty." *A Biographical Dictionary of the Living Authors of Great Britain and Ireland* (London: Henry Colburn, 1816) lists her as follows:

> DACRE, CHARLOTTE, better known by the assumed name of *Rosa Matilda* affixed to some of her publications; born about 1783. Besides many fugitive pieces in the Morning Post newspaper, she has written:
>
> Confessions of the Nun of St. Omers, nov[el] 3 v[ols.] 1805.—Hours of Solitude, poems, 2 v. 8vo. 1805—Zofloya, or the Moor, rom[ance] 12mo. 1806.—The Libertine, nov. 4 v. 1807. 3d. ed. 1809. —The Passions, nov. 4 v. 12mo. 1811.

Burton R. Pollin, in the most recent investigation of her ("Byron, Poe, and Miss Matilda," *Names*, XVI [1968], 390–414), mentions that "Yale has an apparently unique copy of a twenty-eight page novel by 'Miss Dacre,' entitled *The School of Friends, A Domestic Tale* (printed for Thomas Tegg, London, n.d.)," but he gives no evidence to connect this chapbook or this "Miss Dacre" with "Rosa Matilda," though as Montague Summers notes in his Introduction to *Zofloya, or The Moor* (n.d., but ca. 1925; p. xxv), in 1810 Tegg issued a chapbook based on *Zofloya* entitled *The Dæmon of Venice*.

The discussion of Charlotte Dacre's identity revolves

INTRODUCTION

around Byron's mentions of her in various editions of
English Bards and Scotch Reviewers and in the notes added
by E.H. Coleridge to his edition of Byron's *Poetical Works*
([1904], I, 357–358). In the fourth edition (1811), Byron
describes the kinds of minor poetry he will not stoop to
attack, including such satires as *All the Talents* by Eaton
Stannard Barrett (q.v.), and then writes:

> Far be't from me unkindly to upbraid
> The lovely ROSA'S prose in masquerade,
> Whose strains, the faithful echo of her mind,
> Leave wondering comprehension far behind.
> Though Crusca's bards no more our journals fill,
> Some stragglers skirmish round the columns still;
> Last of the howling host which once was Bell's,
> Matilda snivels yet, and Hafiz yells;
> And Merry's metaphors appear anew,
> Chained to the signature of O.P.Q.

> (lines 755–764)

To line 758, Byron added this note (first appearing in the
second edition, October 1809):

> This lovely little Jessica, the daughter of the noted
> Jew King, seems to be a follower of the Della Crusca
> school, and has published two volumes of very re-
> spectable absurdities in rhyme, as times go; besides
> sundry novels in the style of the first edition of *The
> Monk.*

E. H. Coleridge quotes a manuscript note Byron added to
this in 1816: "She has since married the *Morning Post*—an
exceeding good match" and an additional note (which

INTRODUCTION

Coleridge says is "in pencil and, possibly, in another hand"): "and is now dead—which is better," and then the editor writes:

> The novelist "Rosa," the daughter of "Jew King," the lordly money-lender who lived in Clarges Street, and drove a yellow chariot, may possibly be confounded with "Rosa Matilda," Mrs. Byrne (Gronow, *Rem.* (1889), i. 132–136).

Though I have for several years attempted to gather information on John ("Jew") King (b. Jacob Rey, 1753–1824), second husband of Jane Rochfort Butler (the only daughter of the first Earl of Belvedere and widow of Brinsley Butler, second Earl of Lanesborough), nothing I have encountered—least of all the account in Captain Rees Howell Gronow's *Reminiscences* that E. H. Coleridge cites—suggests that King had a daughter named Rosa or a daughter who was a novelist. But King, who was certainly one of the most colorful and, from all accounts, one of the most remarkable London characters of the period and who had direct dealings with Godwin, Byron, and Shelley (as well as with half the British nobility), did have a step-daughter named Charlotte (the fifth child of Lord Lanesborough); this stepdaughter, early in 1806, married Clement Debbieg, son of General Hugh Debbieg (*DNB*), but died on May 19, 1808 (John Debrett, *Peerage of the United Kingdom* [1817], II, 970–972; *Annual Register for 1806*, p. 474). Byron's knowledge of John King's family life must have been superficial, to say the least (see the full text of Byron's account of their acquaintance in Byron, *Letters and Journals,* ed. R. E. Prothero [1903], II, 174–175). But King not only "gave excellent dinners" at his fine home in Clarges Street (later owned by Edward Bulwer Lytton),

INTRODUCTION

attended both by the nobility and by literary figures ranging from Robert Merry, the Della Cruscan poet, Godwin, Holcroft, and Sheridan to John Taylor (later editor of the *Sun* newspaper and author of *Monsieur Tonson*), but he also took his family for a daily ride through fashionable parks in his yellow carriage. More likely, Byron saw and admired Charlotte Butler. Gronow (1794–1865) describes her mother as "a fine-looking woman," though she must have been seventy or seventy-five years old by the time Gronow saw her (she had married Lord Lanesborough in 1754). If Byron was told that Charlotte Butler was the "daughter" of King, the 1806 marriage and death in 1808 of Charlotte Debbieg, combined with misinformation conflating her with Charlotte Dacre, could account for most of the content of Byron's two notes, published and unpublished.

But there remains a mystery. If Byron was confusing Charlotte Butler Debbieg with Charlotte Dacre, then who was "the Morning Post" that she supposedly married— Clement Debbieg or (as Montague Summers states as a fact in his Introduction to *Zofloya*) "William Pitt Byrne, Robinson's successor as editor of the *Morning Post*"? Perhaps Summers tracked down the record of such a marriage, but I can find no evidence that this Byrne was even old enough to have been associated with the *Morning Post* before the date of Byron's note (see *DNB* under Julia Clara Byrne). Rather, it is Nicholas Byrne, the printer, who is thought to have taken over management of the *Morning Post* about 1803 (see Samuel Taylor Coleridge, *Essays on His Times*, ed. David V. Erdman [1978], I, cxvii fn.; S. T. Coleridge, *Notebooks*, ed. Kathleen Coburn, II [1961], #1868 note; Coleridge, *Letters*, ed. E. L. Griggs, III [1959], 50). As Erdman indicates, the real ownership of the *Morning Post* during this period was mysterious in Coleridge's time and remains so today, and perhaps Clem-

INTRODUCTION

ent Debbieg was—or, at least, Byron believed him to be—the owner of the newspaper at this period. In that case, assertions about the identity of Charlotte Dacre's putative husband (insofar as they derive from Byron's note) would be meaningless, and we are reduced to the biographical information available in Dacre's own publications and echoed in the *Biographical Dictionary* of 1816, which mentions neither her marriage nor her death.

There remains even within this narrow range of evidence one other possible problem. Whereas the 1816 *Biographical Dictionary of Living Authors* and most other authorities date the first edition of Dacre's novel *The Libertine* as 1807 (3rd edition, 1809), William S. Ward's valuable *Literary Reviews in British Periodicals, 1798–1820* ([1972], I, 233) lists the first edition of *The Libertine* as having been published anonymously in 1798. If that were true, the only substantial biographical fact I think we still have about Dacre—namely the date of her birth—would be cast in doubt, for then she would have had to publish *The Libertine* at about the age of sixteen. Only a detailed examination of those early reviews, of publishers' lists, and of collections of novels of the period could settle the matter, but I suspect that the 1798 reviews are of a similar work published under the same title (and long forgotten by the time Dacre went to press with her third novel).

Thus we are left (I hope) with Dacre's approximate age and her dedication of *Hours of Solitude* to John Penn, Esq. (*Zofloya,* the only one of Dacre's novels of which I have been able to examine the first edition, contains no dedication or any personal information about the author.) John Penn (1760–1834; *DNB*) was the grandson of William Penn and, by inheritance, co-proprietor of Pennsylvania as well as of Stoke Poges Park in Buckinghamshire. After the success of the American War for Independence, Penn received compensatory settlements for his losses both from the commonwealth of Pennsylvania (£15,000 per year) and from Parliament. He then built a magnificent new home at Stoke Poges (begun 1789), served as sheriff of Buckinghamshire (1798), M.P. for Helston, Cornwall (1802), and governor of the Isle of Portland, Dorset (1805), where he had, shortly before that date, built another mansion. Unless Penn met Charlotte Dacre in London, she probably came, then, either from the area of Stoke Poges north of Slough, in the Thames Valley (and the traditional site of the "country churchyard" of Gray's *Elegy*), or from the Isle of Portland, near Weymouth, Dorset.

Penn must have been something of an eccentric. In 1817 he founded a "matrimonial society" to improve "the domestic life of married persons" (though he himself never married). We cannot know what kind of interest he took in Charlotte Dacre, but from the tenor of her poems, many of which are the laments of betrayed and "fallen" women, we can speculate that Penn may have provided her with financial assistance to support herself while she established herself in a literary career after a period of isolation resulting from a betrayal of love by another man. This hypothesis would explain both the tone and the title of her *Hours of Solitude,* as well as give point to the themes of some of her Gothic fiction. Until we find more solid biographical information, we are left with such tenuous speculations.

We can be certain that Charlotte Dacre's Gothic novels were read avidly by Shelley, who mentions "Rosa Matilda" in his *Letters* (ed. F. L. Jones [1964], I, 120). Thomas Medwin argued that Shelley's own Gothic novels *Zastrozzi* and *St. Irvyne* derive directly from *Zofloya,* an opinion shared by Swinburne, who had read *Zofloya* (see Medwin, *Life of Percy Bysshe Shelley,* ed. H. B. Forman [1913], p. 25 and note). As I mentioned in the Introduction to William

INTRODUCTION

Thomas Fitzgerald's poems, Thomas Moore once played a joke on Byron by pretending to believe that Byron's anonymous *Ode to Napoleon Buonaparte* was written either by Fitzgerald or "Rosa Matilda" (see *Byron's Letters and Journals*, ed. Leslie A. Marchand, IV [1975], 100 fn.; Moore, *Letters and Journals of Lord Byron*, 3rd ed. [1833], II, 58 fn.)

Dacre's *Hours of Solitude*, like Byron's *Hours of Idleness* (1807) and Shelley's early poems preserved in *The Esdaile Notebook* (prepared for publication in 1813, but first published in an edition by Kenneth Neill Cameron in 1964), are overly dramatic and sensationalized in their expression of emotion. They are, moreover, notably free of any hint of the learned classical tradition that had so dominated English poetry from Ben Jonson and Milton through Collins, Gray, and the Wartons. Dacre's poetry—like the tradition of the Gothic novel, in which Dacre followed Ann Radcliffe—in no way attempted to compete with the learned imitations of Horace, Juvenal, or Pindar. It both appealed to and fostered the growing readership made up of women (most of them cursorily educated) and lower-middle-class men, who required reading matter on entirely different principles from the traditional "poetry of allusion" produced by Milton, Pope, and Gray. That Dacre's verses share some basic parallels in subject, language, and tone with the early poems of Byron and Shelley suggests that even those poets with the best Harrow or Eton, Cambridge or Oxford educations were substantially influenced by the shift to egalitarian social and literary values championed by older university men like Wordsworth, Coleridge, and Southey, as well as drawn by the size of this new readership not steeped in the classics. Perhaps the fact that Elizabeth Pigot was one of Byron's first sympathetic readers and that Shelley's coadjutor was his sister Elizabeth

xi

made these poets especially aware of the response of the unlearned audience in their early work. But in any case, the very fact that Charlotte Dacre's fiction and poetry could impress itself on the consciousness of these two well educated aristocrats demonstrates that the barriers between popular and learned culture were falling in England by the first decade of the nineteenth century.

Had Wordsworth, Coleridge, Byron, and Shelley attempted to maintain their positions in a literary aristocracy (as Landor, Wrangham, and Byron's friends Robert Bland and Francis Hodgson succeeded in doing), they would have cut themselves off from the social and ideological currents of their age to such an extent that they could not have developed into the leading poets they became. Just as women poets such as Hemans and lower-class poets such as Bloomfield who lacked the mastery of the past literary tradition were unable to utilize its powerful myths, symbols, and allusions in their work, so those well educated poets who turned their backs on British popular culture (as Thomas Jefferson Hogg and Thomas Love Peacock vainly urged Shelley to do) lost their place in the developments that would make their poetry relevant not only to their contemporaries but to posterity. Just as Keats had to reach up to the classical tradition to find his universal voice, so Byron and Shelley had to reach down to poetry like that of "Rosa Matilda" to find theirs.

Donald H. Reiman

HOURS OF SOLITUDE.

VOL. I.

A. Buck del.   A. Cardon sc.

Rosa Matilda

Published May 18th 1805 by Hughes, Wigmore Street

HOURS OF SOLITUDE.

A COLLECTION OF

Original Poems,

NOW FIRST PUBLISHED.

By CHARLOTTE DACRE,

BETTER KNOWN BY THE NAME OF

ROSA MATILDA.

IN TWO VOLUMES.

VOL. I.

Ah! what is mirth but turbulence unholy,
When to the charm compar'd of heav'nly melancholy?
MILTON.

London:

Printed by D. N. SHURY, Berwick Street, Soho;

FOR HUGHES, WIGMORE STREET, CAVENDISH SQUARE;
AND RIDGEWAY, PICCADILLY.

1805.

To *JOHN PENN, Esq.*

SIR,

TO you, the Patron of literature, and the Friend of mankind, permit me to dedicate the subsequent pages. Part are the production of my untaught youth, and part of my later years. To your valuable hints am I indebted for whatever of correctness or accuracy my labours may boast; to your condescension, in improving my taste; and to your goodness, in calling forth an exertion of the slight talents I may possess. For this let me offer you this public tribute of my gratitude, far, very far inferior to that which is registered in my heart.

I have the honour to be,

SIR,

Your respectful servant and admirer,

CHARLOTTE DACRE.

Signed Charlotte Dacre Author of the "Confessions of the Nun of St Omer's"

TO THE PUBLIC.

———————————

THOSE Poems in the subsequent collection, where the age at which they were written is not mentioned at the head, are of a recent date. At the age of three-and-twenty, therefore, having no longer extreme youth to plead in extenuation of their errors, I must merely recommend them to mercy.

HOURS OF SOLITUDE.

THE TRIUMPH OF PLEASURE*.

(*Written at Sixteen.*)

BEAUTY reclin'd beneath the shade;
Blooming Health before her play'd;
Her golden tresses kissed the wind.
Meek Content, with placid mind,
Her wreath of fadeless flowers entwin'd.
Peace and Virtue join'd the round ;
Innocence their fav'rite crown'd ;

---

* Having lately heard that the above Poem bore some re-
semblance to " The Female Seducers," I think it necessary to
state, that I never perused it till curiosity, at this observation,
induced me to do so. I do not think the remark a just one.

Youth's bright fire illum'd her eye,
And gave her cheeks their vermeil dye.
Sudden strange thoughts attack her rest,
Perplexing visions pain her breast;
The chains of Morpheus burst in twain,
And Love approach'd with glitt'ring train.
Beauty waking, gaz'd around;
Cupid, laughing, kiss'd the ground:
" Fairest virgin, haste away,
Come with me to joyful day;
Sleep no more in realms of night,
Come with me and taste delight;
Refuse me not—my name is Love,
Fav'rite of the gods above.
Fairest maid, then haste away,
And come with me to joyous day!"

He said, and slily strung his bow,
    The arrow sought to hide:
A wither'd hand receives the blow,
    And turns the dart aside.

'Twas Age the timely freedom took.
Cupid stamp'd with frowning look.

Age regardless pass'd him by,
On Beauty gaz'd, and heav'd a sigh.

" Virgin, shun your treach'rous guide ;
   I once was fair like you :
Love from me in vain would hide—
   His joys are most untrue."

   The maiden sigh'd as Age went on :
" I tell thee, life is quickly gone ;
Pale Experience robs the scene
Of Fancy's fadeless evergreen,
Steals the lamp of Love away,
And shews it cloth'd in sober grey.
Love, disgusted, stays no more,
Spreads his wings, and flies fourscore.
Think, oh, think! that youthful bloom,
Waits not even for the tomb !
Time will dim those lust'rous eyes ;
The dart of Death resistless flies :
Turn, fair daughter, and be wise !
All is misery, grief, and shame,
Pleasure lives not but in name.

Trust me, Love is mere deceit—
Snakes, not roses, 'twine his feet;

" Pain, not Pleasure, is his guest,
  Jealousy, by furies nurs'd,
Dark Revenge, with bloody crest,
  Gall-fill'd Envy, nearly burst,
Black Suspicion's basilisk eye,
Sharp-tooth'd Slander's cunning lie,
Foaming Rage, and grinning Spite,
Mischief sly, that shuns the light.
Pleasure ! 'tis a term for folly,
Ending soon in melancholy ;
Sad repentance keeps her side,
And blushing shame, that fain would hide.
Hope no joy, then, meets you there,
But, plunging in a sea of care,
Nothing, nothing but despair.

" Fare thee well! my power must end ;
I give the warning of a friend—
My time expires—no more I dare."—
Then mingled with th' absorbent air.

Pensive Beauty gaz'd around ;
 Her cheeks were wet with tears ;
And thus, with trembling dew-trops crown'd,
 The morning rose appears.

 Love in grief now sidelong turn'd,
His zealous heart with fury burn'd,
His drooping wings despondent hung,
And useless bow was backward flung ;
But yet, resolv'd his power to try,
With sweet persuasion in each eye,
Once more his bloomy lips divide,
While countless dimples laugh beside:

 " Weep no more, fair-bosom'd maid,
Those eyes are not for tears to shade !
Frosty Age no pleasure knows—
Youth and Age have long been foes ;
The leafless tree again shall bloom,
But Age is beauty's final tomb ;
Chearless Winter's ice-clad brow
Relaxes in young Summer's glow,
But Age no second spring can know.

Come then, fairest, come with me,
Mirth and smiles shall wait on thee!"

He mark'd young Beauty's heaving breast,
And eyes that all her soul confess'd—
Saw their bright'ning beams displace
The clouds that erst o'erspread her face,
While sparkling tears no more remain
Than dew-drops on the sunny plain.

Cupid's graceful wings rose high—
He bade his dang'rous train come nigh.
Swift the glitt'ring throng advance,
Twining in a mystic dance:
Rapture, Hope, fond Doubt, and Joy
Kneel before the Cyprian boy;
Pleasure led the jocund rear,
Smiling arch with wanton leer;
Her master's beck she ran to meet,
Poppies springing 'neath her feet.
Soft he seiz'd her polish'd arm;
Scarce the nymph conceal'd a charm;
Poppies crown'd her raven hair
Which wanton'd o'er her shoulders fair;

Ringlets 'twin'd her vaulted brow,
And sought to hide her breast of snow ;
Seduction lurk'd in every sigh,
And fascination in her eye.
Beauty blush'd, her gaze withdrew,
Nor durst the shameless syren view.
Her right hand held a blooming wreath,
But many thorns were hid beneath ;
Her left, a polish'd glass display'd,
Through which appear'd a sunny glade ;
Beyond, serene the ocean curl'd,
And show'd a trembling, wat'ry world :
There, stretch'd a plain of smoothest green,
Where many serpents lurk'd unseen ;
And roseate bowers allur'd the eye,
Where ambush'd Treach'ry deep did lie.
Reclining here, beneath the shade
Sleeps a languid, half-dress'd maid;
There, a youth, whose varying cheek,
Seems disorder to bespeak ;
Some painful dream disturbs his rest,
And heaves with sighs his lab'ring breast.
He sees, perhaps, the visions fade
Which erst his wand'ring feet betray'd.

Joining in the noisy rout,
What listless numbers dance about!
There, Laughter and her revel throng
Shake the air with clam'rous song,
While some contemn the outrag'd day,
And dream their sickly lives away.

Strange, such delusion should have charms
To lure fresh victims to her arms!
Yet Beauty gaz'd and gaz'd again,
While Pleasure mark'd her struggling pain.
So the fell snake attracts the eye,
Then bids the wretch entangled die.

And now her silver voice essay'd
At once to fix the varying maid :
" See," she cried, with magic grace,
" Gaze on yon enchanting place!
Charms not thee their airy sport?
There live the vassals of my court :
Thou shalt be the fairest there,
Their idol and their only care.
Anxious now they wait thy charms—
Shall I waft thee to their arms?"

Deluded Beauty eager gaz'd,
Half her sylph-like form she rais'd;
When lo! a noble youth she spied,
Who hung his head and deeply sigh'd.
Pale was his cheek, yet softest grace
Illumin'd his dejected face;
Beauteous dimples watch'd his smile,
The sense to seize, the heart to guile.
The fair one gaz'd, forgot the snare,
And left her guardless bosom bare.
Watching Cupid seiz'd his dart,
And shot triumphant through her heart!
Swift poison tingled in her veins,
Her breast throbb'd wild with nameless pains;
The more she look'd, the more she fir'd,
Nor knew 'twas Love her soul inspir'd.

Sudden she caught the wand'rer's eye;
His cheeks assum'd a crimson dye,
His glance was fierce, impassion'd high;
Dissolv'd-he seem'd in amorous fire,
Yielding his soul to soft desire.
Eager with love he view'd the fair,
Stretching his arms on vacant air;

Then kneeling, trembling, kiss'd the ground—
Tho' conqueror, seem'd a captive bound.
She rose, in brilliant blushes drest,
Reclin'd her head on Pleasure's breast;
Falt'ring whisper'd, " I am thine—
Take me, goddess, to thy shrine !"
Pleasure arch at Cupid smil'd,
He laugh'd to see the maid beguil'd.
Each seiz'd an hand.   Oh, Reason, mourn !
Beauty by Love and Pleasure borne !
With their gods the pageant train
Rose, dazzling visions, false and vain ;
But Beauty's train hung low the head,
Nor follow'd where the meteors led.
She, sailing joyful on the wind,
Leaving irradiant Truth behind,
Is wafted to that fatal shore
Where Virtue sinks " to rise no more."

THE EXILE.

*Composed on the sea-shore, and founded on the fate of
an unfortunate Female born to better hopes.*

(Written at Sixteen.)

SWEEP on, ye winds—congenial billows roar,
As, lost, I wander on your dubious shore ;
In sad review each shudd'ring vision see
Pass slow along, and turn their looks on me ;
See pale Experience with her sadden'd eye
Gaze on the shades, and hear her hollow sigh ;
Bless the relentless gloom that weighs the air,
And hail it, fit associate of Despair.

Dark as my fate the prospect round me low'rs,
As, rob'd in sadness, pass my pensive hours.
The past, a dream—the future, wrapt in shade,
Vainly to pierce my soul has oft essay'd ;

To dim perspective hast'ning shadows fly,
And veil'd in mist, my straining gaze defy,
Or, like mysterious pageants, mock the eye ;
In wild conjecture sinks my boding heart,
For fate in ambush still suspends her dart.

The day's drear aspect, when I first drew breath,
Foretold a blight to shrink my hopes with death ;
Dark rose the morn, from Heaven's awful gate
Wept the full clouds, as though they mourn'd my fate ;
Nor was the eve in one bright ray attir'd,
But chill and sad the grievous day retir'd—
Prophetic day! too well didst thou express
That woe unvarying must my life oppress !
The morn *has* pass'd ; the day still wastes in gloom,
Till deep'ning comes the darkness of the tomb.

O welcome, tomb! I fondly look to thee,
As wearied mariners a port from sea;
Thou bid'st alone the shackled wretch be free.
Despair flies vanquish'd from the gates of death,
And cedes his empire with the parting breath.
There can no tyrant free-born minds enslave,
For human pow'r is *pow'rless* o'er the grave.

Ah! what avails it then the chance that sped?
Whether 'twas virtue, hope, or fancy led
The dazz'ling visions of the wand'rer's head:
Whether the dupe of all, or slave of love,
Or wild enthusiast, only skill'd to rove:
Whether the child of error or of fate,
Ah! what avails the folly of debate?

And now, great God! to thee forlorn I pray—
Teach me to struggle through my arduous day!
Let me not sink ignobly 'neath the scorn
Of narrow minds, or wretches vulgar born,
But from their *pity* doubly spare my mind—
Cheap, humbling pity of the mock-refin'd!
Let me from added evil still arise,
Like the proud flame aspiring to the skies,
Or freedom, struggling with an host of foes,
That more elastic from oppression grows!
Ah! let me not, whatever be my doom,
Involve *another* in its fatal gloom!
Let none accuse me with the harrowing name
Of base destroyer of *their* peace or fame;
In secret let my anguish'd bosom swell,
In secret all my faults and sorrows dwell!

Hope flies alarm'd from sorrows such as mine,
And back recoils the powerless hand of Time :
'Tis Death alone, stalking with pride elate,
The king of time, the conqueror of fate,
Smiles on me now, while struggling through the gloom,
And marks me, in proud triumph, for the tomb.

Then soon farewell for ever, friend or foe!
Indifferent to love or hate I go.
Farewell, oh, *man!* destroyer of my fame!
Forgot for ever be my injur'd name!
'Tis your unkindness digs my early grave,
Prone to destroy, with every power to save.
No more my just, though slighted claims appear ;
Hush then your *conscience*, 'tis *her* voice you hear.
Those many wrongs that owe to you their birth,
Like restless spirits, ever scare your mirth ;
Still, while you sleep, in dreams your mind shall roll,
And cries for vengeance dimly wake your soul ;
Thine offspring hear, unown'd upon thee call—
In sad disgrace they share their mother's fall ;
Unpitied, roaming in the world, they find
No chance of life but preying on mankind ;

Till, desperately just, their country's laws
Doom an ignoble death, nor scan the cause;
Justice denies what Mercy would require,
And for a nation's good, see, they expire!

Yes, thou fond lover of thy vices, see
Their end who liv'd and are destroy'd by thee!
(Tormenting thought, destroy'd by *thee* to say!)
Ah! tempt no more the blood-besprinkled way;
Reform, and swift thy ruthless crimes deplore,
For in the grave repentance is no more.

Now summer fades upon the sterner year,
That conqu'ring comes with aspect sad and drear.
Fly not, sweet season! yet a little stay,
And gild with genial beams my lonely day.
'Tis such as I should mark, with sadden'd eye,
In sad progression all thy beauties die;
Should mark the fading of thy smile serene,
And linger hopeless o'er thy with'ring green.
Oh! where, (for this enervates me with dread,)
Oh! where in *winter* shall I rest my head?
No home, no shelter in the expanse drear,
No friend, no family have I to cheer.

A niggard sum, in trembling anguish told,
Speaks, to a day, how long my life I hold.
When *this* is gone—ah! what the fate decreed—
Famine must waste, or suicide bid me bleed.

Yet ere that day shall not sweet hope be mine ?
Outstep destruction with a speed divine?
Shall I not *yet* reject the fatal steel,
And gratitude for godlike mercy feel?
No, no—'tis fix'd—vain tears, no longer flow,
For happiness I ne'er shall meet below.

Oh! thou, devoid of honour! but for thee,
I still would breathe the life of nature, free—
Still tranquil, for still *pure*, my hours had been,
Not faded in their earliest transient green.
So the young rose, of gentle summer born,
I've seen expanding to the orient morn ;
Then Zephyr courts it ; but not long its term
Of splendour, hasten'd by the cank'ring worm.
Like me it falls, ere half its little day,
And leaves at large the ravager to prey.

ELOQUENCE.

Addressed to a gentleman who eloquently maintained
that Love, if analysed, was Folly.

(Written at fifteen.)

AVAUNT thee, soft Eloquence, exquisite harm!
  Nor longer thy poison impart,
Nor longer endeavour, thou dangerous charm,
  To lure Sensibility's heart.

Oh! first-born of Harmony! sister to Love!
  Partaking its flow'rs and its thorn ;
Now bidding the sad heart tumultuously move,
  Then shewing its fond hopes as forlorn.

Thou canst soothe the pale mourner by sorrow opprest,
  Bring comfort on Pity's fair wings ;
Thou canst lull the poor penitent's struggles to rest,
  And disarm even pain of its stings.

And Music, what rapture thy melody brings,
    What thrillings the bosom inspire,
If the sweet hand of Sentiment sweep o'er the strings,
    Or Love sound the tremulous lyre!

Though thy magic give ease to the agonis'd wounds
    Of Love, by the canker of care ;
And tho', lur'd by the wonderful skill of thy sounds,
    Hope should rise from the tomb of Despair :—

Yet, Music, tho' none may thy powers deny,
    In chasing Love's deep melancholy,
'Tis Eloquence bids thee despairing go die,
    And shews us e'en *Love is a Folly*.

PASSION UNINSPIRED BY SENTIMENT.

Addressed to him who denied their existing together.

OH! Passion, seducer of heart and of soul!
　Thou transport tyrannic! half pleasure, half pain!
Why consum'st thou the breast with such madd'ning
　　　controul?
　Fly quickly—yet, ah! come as quickly again.

Without thee, what's life but a wilderness drear,
　Or a chill, gloomy vale, where stern apathy reigns?
Like Phœbus, thy vivid refulgence can cheer,
　And brighten, in rapture, e'en Memory's pains.

When pleasure seduces the wild throbbing heart
　In moments ecstatic of tender excess,
When Fancy refines, and when Passion takes part,
　The lover existence too fondly may bless.

Yet Passion alone, to the delicate mind,
  Aspires not a simple *sensation* above ;
Unless sentiment yield it an ardour refin'd,
  It degrades, not ennobles the essence of love.

To JOHN PENN, Esq.

I joy to see that still on earth
  The sympathetic sigh
Can in a human heart find birth,
  Or pity dim the eye.

For long I thought all feeling gone;
  Disgust had seiz'd my heart:
I view'd the selfish world with scorn,
  But pride conceal'd my smart—

And men beyond conception base,
  And women false and vain:
My wand'ring heart ne'er found a place,
  Cast back on me again.

From such a world alarm'd I fly,
  In solitude to pine;
I *feel*, but will in secret die,
  And guard *those* feelings mine.

THE KISS.

THE greatest bliss
Is in a kiss—
A kiss of love refin'd,
  When springs the soul
  Without controul,
And blends the bliss with mind.

For if desire
Alone inspire,
The kiss not *me* can charm ;
  The eye must beam
  With *chasten'd* gleam
That would *my* soul disarm.

What fond delight
Does love excite
When sentiment takes part!
The falt'ring sigh,
Voluptuous eye,
And palpitating heart.

Ye fleet too fast—
Sweet moments, last
A little longer mine!
Like Heaven's bow
Ye fade—ye go;
Too tremulously fine!

THE VANITY OF HOPE.

SINCE to hope for true love is but folly,
   And woman's the plaything of man,
My soul sinks in deep melancholy,
   Corroding my life's little span.

Oh! I wish my sad eyes could discover
   A being of nature refin'd,
What rapture to prove him a lover,
   A lover of sensitive mind!

But such, in this world, to my sorrow,
   I never can hope to attain,
For this day shall pass on and the morrow,
   And my wishes will still be in vain.

For the fancy of man ever turning,
  Affection he well can withhold;
And his *Passions*, though ardently burning,
  Leave his *Heart* unaffected and cold.

Then in solitude still let me languish,
  Contempt brace the nerves of my mind,
Indiff'rence preserve me from anguish,
  And despair to the wind be consign'd.

TO HIM WHO SAYS HE LOVES.

YOU tell me that you truly love :
  Ah ! know you well what love does mean?
Does neither whim nor fancy move
  The rapture of your transient dream ?

Tell me, when absent do you think
  O'er ev'ry look and ev'ry sigh?
Do you in melancholy sink,
  And hope and doubt you know not why?

When present, do you die to say
  How much you love, yet fear to tell?
Does her breath melt your soul away?
  A touch, your nerves with transport swell?

Or do you faint with sweet excess
   Of pleasure rising into pain,
When hoping you may e'er possess
   The object you aspire to gain ?

The charms of every other fair
   With coldness could you learn to view?
Fondly unchang'd to her repair,
   With transports ever young and new?

Could you, for her, fame, wealth despise?
   In poverty and toil feel blest?
Drink sweet delusion from her eyes,
   Or smile at ruin on her breast?

And tell me, at her loss or hate,
   Would *death* your only refuge prove?
Ah! if in aught you hesitate,
   Coward! you dare not say you love.

THE ANSWER,

By George Skeene, Esq. as it appeared in the Morning Herald.

FULL well I know what love does mean,
  Full well its force and tyranny,
And captive in love's chains have been
  Since first I set my eyes on thee.

No fancy, whim, or idle dream,
  To love like mine could e'er give birth,
Which, flowing from the purest stream,
  Owns, for its source, superior worth.

The angel form of her I love
  Reflects the beauty of her mind,
Where all the virtues sweetly move,
  In joy and harmony combin'd.

Bless'd with *her* love, all other charms
  With coldness I could learn to view,
And in the heaven of her arms
  Taste raptures ever young and new.

For her, could fame and wealth despise,
  In poverty and toil feel blest,
Drink sweet delusion from her eyes,
  Or smile at ruin on her breast.

But to endure her loss or hate
  All human efforts would be vain;
No balm could heal, no charms abate,
  Or soothe such agony of pain.

Vain world, adieu! in fervent pray'r
  I'd bless her with my latest breath,
And, robb'd of all my soul held dear,
  Seek refuge in the arms of death.

LOVE AND MADNESS.

OVER the moor a lady fair
 Took her way so sadly;
Her face was pale, her bosom bare,
 Sweet she sung, though madly :

" I had a lover once, believe me,
 His blue eyes shone so mildly ;
He's gone, and can I choose but grieve me?
 He's lost, and I wander wildly.

" Stranger, do not look on me!
 What would you discover?
I had a serpent sister—she
 It was who stole my lover.

" Stranger, do not weep for *me!*
 I am past complaining;
The struggle that you think you see
 Is pride my love disdaining.

" But this struggle will not last,
 Not beyond to-morrow ;
Life's idle hour I pass so fast,
 I leave behind my sorrow.

" Farewell, stranger—now farewell!
 Here I cannot ponder—
Hark, I hear the warning bell !
 Death is waiting yonder.

" In dim perspective, see, oh ! see
 His shadowy figure bending
O'er a small spot meant for me—
 Round pale ghosts attending."

Sudden she turn'd, her wounded mind
 With wilder frenzy firing—
" Farewell!" linger'd on the wind,
 My soul with grief inspiring.

Maniac sweet! I do not know,
   Though sad thy lot and dreary,
If happier still thou art not, so,
   Than of *reas'ning sorrows* weary.

THE FOLLY OF LIFE.

AND what is life? A fleeting shade,
A cheerless, beamless, frozen glade,
A span too short for joy to smile,
Ere restless hopes and fears beguile—
   A nervous, feverish dream, at best,
     From which the wise desire
    To wake, then sink to endless rest,
     And *gratefully* expire.

With calm disdain, compos'd, resign'd,
The greatly philosophic mind
Can view with firm, unshrinking eye,
The tyrant pale and grim come nigh ;
   Can view him with a smile of scorn,
     Sigh, and remember still,
    True, true the grave is cold, forlorn,
     But man's heart colder still.

Yet grov'ling on their misty way,
And led perpetually astray,
The wretched universal mind
Seem to their sickly life resign'd ;
　　And meanly toiling on, thro' fear,
　　　　Would shudder could they see
　　The million dangers lurking near,
　　　　Afraid of what *may be.*

Yet not afraid of *present ills,*
'Tis apprehension only kills.
The dastard soul, abas'd and mean,
Ephemeral, sports in the beam.
　　Hereafter pales the coward cheek,
　　　　While folly rules the day,
　　And, base, contemptible, and weak,
　　　　He prays but for delay.

Poor mortal, 'tis not giv'n to thee
Immaculate, or great to be :
Yet, far as *power* will permit,
Be just, humane—to ills submit ;

Be firm, be noble, and preserve
   An *independent* mind,
From honour's path forbear to swerve,
   Look up, and die resign'd.

THE UNFAITHFUL LOVER.

(IMPROMPTU.)

How dare you say that *still* you love?
  In truth you'll move my rage,
Or, likelier far, my *scorn* you'll prove,
  If deeper you engage.

Be warn'd, in time, *I* love no more,
  Nor can I ever change:
One pang I felt, but now 'tis o'er,
  And *you* may freely range.

Cold, cold I feel to all your sighs,
  Cold, cold to all your tears,
Indiff'rence arms my alter'd eyes,
  And apathy my ears.

Hard as the flinty rock I seem ;
   The form no longer charms,
That, wand'ring in a fev'rish dream,
   Dwelt in the *wanton*'s arms.

Go, satiate there—*my* love so pure
   Shall never more be yours ;
Let meretricious charms allure,
   And wing your worthless hours.

Seduction from those eyes no more
   My conscious nerves will feel ;
And while your sorrows I deplore,
   I have no *wish* to heal.

I know another *still* might say
   Your *heart* remain'd her own ;
I think the *senses* cannot stray
   Indiff'rent and alone :

For 'tis the senses that delude,
   That vitiate the *heart;*
Refinement dies as they intrude,
   And *love* conceals his dart.

Your *friend* perhaps I still may be—
Your mistress, never, never;
The flame that dazzled you from me
Leaves you more lost than ever.

THE MOTHER TO HER DYING INFANT.

" Die, my love—I'll not regret thee—
  Die, and me of hope bereave :
If thou liv'st, what ills beset thee !
  Die, and never know to grieve,

" Soft, my angel ; calmly sleeping,
  Sleep thy guiltless life away ;
Leave to me the task of weeping,
  That, with thine, ends not my day.

But, oh ! forbear that smile soul-riving—
  Smile not, strugg'ling for thy breath !
Smile not, in the conflict striving—
  Life beseeching *ruthless* death!

" My soul unnerves ; my heart, retreating,
　　Breaks to see that fev'rish glow ;
The hand of terror stays its beating,
　　Lovely angel, look not so !

" Shall these eyes no more behold thee ?
　　Cruel friends, oh, let me stay !
In my arms will I enfold thee
　　Till thou freeze my living clay.

" Sympathetic, softly stealing,
　　Thou *my* heart shalt undermine ;
My warmth to *thine* no warmth revealing,
　　But thy *cold* shall pierce through mine.

" Thy little arms my throat surrounding,
　　Stiffly there shall long remain,
Till time our *mutual* dust confounding,
　　We vegetate on earth again

" Now convulsions swiftly seize thee,
　　Yet, my life, my angel, stay ;
Death alone can e'er release thee,
　　Friends, oh, bear me not away !

" Wretch ! what feelings now possess thee?
   Selfish mother, let him go;
Does his happiness distress thee,
   Mother of unworthy woe?

" Little corpse, of spotless beauty,
   Soon corruption shall thee taint ;
Say for thee I did my duty—
   Tell me that, oh, infant saint!

' Childless wretch, thy hopes are over ;
   Little baby, thou art blest!
I, a solitary rover,
   Know no peace till endless rest."

THE MUSING MANIAC.

(*Written at eighteen.*)

Say, where am I? Can you tell?
  Is my heart within my breast?
Am I bound in magic spell,
  Or by fiends of hell possest?

Say, what horror sways this brain?
  Do I sleep, or do I wake?
If I sleep—oh, dream of pain!
  From my lids thy fetters take.

If within the silent grave
  Once I could but find my way,
Death might pity on me have;
  Rattling with him let me play.

From the sockets of his eyes
    Bid me the grim worm obtain ;
Laughing then to see my prize,
    Place it in its cave again.

Sometimes from my earthy bed
    Bid me dance with spectres wan ;
Why not gambol with the dead,
    And be happy as we can?

Then, at midnight, from the tomb
    Dimly steal, and silent stray,
Snatch a beam, to light the gloom,
    From yonder moon now laughing gay.

Haunt the base with visions dire,
    From their bosoms tear the heart,
Bid them in a dream expire,
    Then awake to *real* smart.

Roaming thus where'er we list,
    Dancing round and dancing round,
Sail upon the shadowy mist,
    Or roll the stars upon the ground.

Thus to sport, and thus to play,
　　Never should I more know care ;
I'll bribe the ghosts that guard the way,
　　And slily soon to death repair.

THE EMIGRANT.

Oh! I shall ne'er forget thee, wretched wight!
  While memory holds forget thee shall I never;
Thy *conscious* form, that shunn'd the garish light,
  The tatter'd garb, that mock'd thy vain endeavour:

Thy pallid cheek, which meagre want had worn,
  And reckless pluck'd the rose of health *once* blooming,
The sunken eye, where dignity and scorn
  Yet sat, to check the rabble's vile presuming—

The sunken eye, that mark'd me as I pass'd,
  Oh, I shall ne'er forget the look soul-wounding!
'Twas pitiful, yet *greatly* sad its cast,
  It struck upon my heart, with folly bounding.

Expression *various* in that look was seen ;
 At once 'twas proud, and *yet* it was imploring ;
Something of stern contempt, and grief between ;
 The *man* was sunk, but yet his *soul* was soaring.

My eyes were fix'd in contemplation sad,
 While he, poor soul! his thin hand faintly raising
O'er a wide rent which cruel time had made,
 Sought to conceal it from my pensive gazing.

Instinctive pride!—Oh, Man! when *truly* great,
 Not e'en adversity the soul's high feeling
Can ever blunt; but, ling'ring with thy fate,
 It still exists, and still it mocks, concealing.

A momentary fire illum'd his eye,
 A pale, pale blush his sallow cheek o'erspreading ;
He pass'd me with a sad and falt'ring sigh,
 Wishful to speak, but yet rebuke seem'd dreading.

Palsying the best emotions of the heart,
 Thou tyrant, Custom! how I *loath* thy folly !
Lest sneering Ignorance should fling her dart
 I durst not soothe this wretch's melancholy.

Perhaps on some cold stone his head to lie
  He slowly pass'd, in secret so despairing,
Alone to wander, or alone to die,
  Perhaps scarce knowing whither, perhaps not caring.

THE MOUNTAIN VIOLET.

(Written at seventeen.)

Sweet fragile flow'r, that bloom'st unsought,
   And bloom'st unseen by many an eye,
Thy charms awake my pensive thought;
   And wake reflexion's bitter sigh.

Thy lowly head with patience bent,
   Unshelter'd, to the northern blast,
As fiercely by the whirlwinds rent,
   Nor deign'd to crush thee as they past;

Expanding wild, thy rich perfume
   Impregnates round the unhallow'd air,
That, reckless of thy virgin bloom,
   Sweeps not o'er thee more mild or fair.

Now brighten'd by the morning ray,
  Luxuriant spreads thy grateful breast ;
Now evening comes, with tyrant sway,
  And chills thy little form to rest.

Sweet emblem of the soul-fraught mind,
  Expos'd life's keenest storms to bear ;
Yet, like thee, tenderly refin'd,
  And shrinking from ungenial air.

The ray which gilds with lucid gleam
  Is innate peace, which none can wrest ;
The evening chill that shrouds the beam,
  The sad reflexions of the breast.

Like thee, too, from the vulgar eye
  The chasten'd mind shall live forlorn ;
For though no kindred soul may sigh,
  In solitude there's none to scorn.

Dear flow'r, be thou my fav'rite sweet !
  I'll rear with care thy drooping head,
Save thy soft breast from heedless feet,
  And court young zephyrs to thy bed.

Yet if perchance, in evil hour,
   Some lawless hand invade thy shrine,
Or nightly blast, with ruthless pow'r,
   Sap the short life which might be thine—

Ah, then, with true regret I'll kneel,
   And try thy beauties dimm'd to chear;
When, ah! if vain my hopes I feel,
   I'll, dead, embalm thee with a tear.

THE LOVER'S VISION.

I lay reclin'd,
And weary of my fate,
With joy I would have chang'd my wretched state;
When on the wind,
A lady beautifully fair,
As fancy has pourtray'd us angels are,
Appear'd with majesty to sail,
And wafted on ambrosial air—
Delicious odours made my senses fail.

I knew my love;
Her face was snowy white,
Her garments streams of undulating light;
Her hair did rove
Loose o'er her slim, irradiant form;
Her look, methought, was freezing and forlorn.
No more did lustre in her eyes abound;
Rays did her head adorn,
Which sparkling coruscations threw around.

" Remember well

How oft thou didst inspire

Glances, tho' chasten'd, yet of ardent fire ;

And now I tell,

Fearing *thy* love were boyish or untrue,

I durst not *mine* in all its fervor shew ;

But now my unfetter'd soul,

Soaring in regions new,

May own its mortal love without controul."

" Oh, thou !" I cried,

And stretch'd my longing arms—

" Oh, why in *life* didst thou withhold thy charms ?

Why, shadowy bride,

While I am living clay,

Speak'st thou of heav'n, yet leadest not the way ?

Let me, bright saint, no more despair,

But take my soul away,

And mix with thine in death, oh, spirit fair !"

With mournful sigh

The beauteous sprite replied :

" Behold around, with deep'ning crimson dy'd,

The eastern sky :

I can no longer *here* remain."
And, as she spoke, more luminous became
    Her form of silv'ry mist.
    Slow it dispers'd.   My eyes in vain
To trace it in the air would still persist.

EXPERIENCE.

(Written at eighteen.)

Ah! wo the hour when fancy held her sway,
  And reason came not with her radiance bright,
When passion flam'd the meteor of the day,
  And blinded, not directed, with its light.

Ah! then, unmindful of the vengeful shade,
  In dim perspective boding to destroy,
I pleas'd my fancy, and my heart it paid,
  Of ev'ry hope, the price for present joy.

For, ah! too soon in sad despair I found
  The gem gay sparkling in the fairy night,
When pale Experience shed her beams around,
  Appear'd a worthless pebble to the sight—

Which Reason, blushing, felt asham'd to own,
  Vex'd to have slumber'd on inactive wing.
But vain regret, nor can the shame atone ;
  The deed, long past, shall leave a length'ning sting.

THE VISIONS OF FANCY.

(*Written at sixteen.*)

As on a rock's stern brow entranc'd I lay,
  The deaf'ning surges bursting at my feet,
Light Fancy at my head assum'd the sway,
  And backward bade the jarring world retreat.

Now shadowy forms with antics glide along,
  Or merrily sailing through the misty air,
The shrill wild echo of their noisy song
  Breaks in strange periods on my sleepy ear.

In dim perspective now a group appear,
  Twining with gambols in a mystic dance;
The aching eye in vain would bring them near,
  They now in shade retreat, and now advance.

Pursu'd by Poverty, Disease, and Care,
   An haggard shade stalks slow along the gloom,
Her thin hands clasp'd upon her bosom bare,
   Mis'ry her name—she seeks the peaceful tomb.

But ah! who rushes from yon mountain brow,
   With wild eyes straining on the vacant air,
Half naked, and with hair dishevel'd so,
   Fix'd in that look of horror? 'Tis Despair.

And next a wretch, most grievous to behold,
   Tearing his bosom with ensanguin'd hands,
Now parch'd with heat appears—now froze with cold:
   'Tis Madness, that on mischief eager stands.

With blood-stain'd dagger, heaving broken sighs,
   A gory vision swims before my sight—
Remorseless Suicide, with tearless eyes,
   Turning on his own breast the weapon bright.

Last, a pale youth that in deep anguish seems,
   Whose heart heaves near to burst his lab'ring breast;
From his dull eye no spark of pleasure gleams,
   For, ah! 'tis *love* has robb'd him of his rest.

Poor youth! too darkly frowns thy stubborn fate,
 For Mis'ry with her rueful train draws near:
"Fly, thou blind victim!" Ah! it proves too late—
 She comes, and fell Destruction in her rear.

He slowly lags, nor *once* of danger thinks;
 To his devoted breast th' oppressor clings:
Lo, on the youth a weight of horror sinks,
 And black around Despondence spreads her wings.

Assaulted Reason totters on her throne;
 Madness usurps the kingdom of the brain;
Death seems the refuge—instant death alone
 His desperate passport to release from pain.

Vainly his drooping soul to chear he tries,
 Vainly attempts to struggle with despair;
On his sad ear resound loud piteous cries,
 And Desolation flaps the desart air.

Now Suicide comes, shaking his dagger high,
 And, smiling ghastly, gives his breast a wound;
Wild rapture lighten'd in the victim's eye,
 And up the dizzying height I saw him bound.

Careless he rush'd through the deep, dang'rous gloom,

  His lips, convuls'd, seem'd mercy to invoke;

I, viewing, agoniz'd, his fatal doom,

  Stretch'd forth my arms to save him—and awoke *.

---

* I have in my possession many more Poems attempted at the early ages of sixteen and seventeen, but do not presume to intrude more of them upon the liberality of my readers.

THE MURDERER.

Silent he stalk'd, and ever and anon
He shudder'd, and turn'd back, saying, " Who fol-
    lows?"
Horror had blanch'd his cheek; his writhing brow
Confess'd the inward struggles of his mind.
E'en in the distant, ever-varying clouds
His tortur'd fancy form'd a vengeful angel,
Pointing the sword of justice o'er his head;
And e'en the murm'ring zephyrs, rushing by,
Seem'd the low whisp'rings of the restless shade
His sanguinary steel had forc'd abroad.

With folded arms, and hesitating tread,
The guilty murd'rer shunn'd the beaten path,
And turn'd where trackless Desolation frown'd.
Now the last crimson tint of eve expir'd,
And fainter grew the vivid western clouds;
The mountains their gigantic shadows threw
Across the boundless plain outstretch'd below;
The blue mists gather'd on their low'ring heads,
And in the dusk delusive shapes uncouth
Cheated the wretched culprit's coward eye.
Vainly for refuge in himself he sought,
For dark remorse and shudd'ring guilt were there,
Despair, and doubts of heaven.   Dark as his fate
Increasing night came on.   The wand'rer sunk
Exhausted down, but sleep disdain'd her snowy plumes
　　　to soil
By hov'ring near the blood-stain'd murd'rer's couch,
And fled to " lids of innocence and peace * "
In agony the prostrate wretch remain'd,
His eyes distended and by madness glaz'd;
Visions of horror shock'd his straining sight.
Now gliding slow he mark'd the angry spirit

* Young.

Of his murder'd friend, which, as it pass'd
In mournful guise, its threat'ning finger shook.
Then came a form most hideous to behold,
Of sable hue, and eyes of sparkling fire.
It stopp'd and grinn'd a smile of triumph, such
As hell alone could shew, and th' arch fiend wear,
Elate, and glorying in the crimes of Man!
Thus harass'd and appall'd, the guilty soul
No hope of *mèrcy* chear'd. His bursting eyes,
On vacancy fierce stretch'd, seem'd wild to scan
Futurity, to him a dread abyss,
A darkly-yawning gulf, within whose womb
Horror-struck Fancy form'd chaotic scenes,
Where fiends malignant various racks prepar'd
To stretch his tortur'd frame, and, agoniz'd,
Wring from his heart, by torment exquisite,
The secret of his murder. Drop by drop
Forc'd from his swelling veins the blood he saw ;
Ten thousand pangs assail'd him ; while around
Terrific yells and laughter seem'd to ring,
With taunts such as the scoffing demons shout
O'er those whom they betray.—Visions so drear,
Compounded by remorseful fancy's sway,
What reason could sustain ? Yet reason still

Maintain'd her seat—the more the murd'rer's woe.
Now from the shadowy gulf, emerging slow,
The King of Terrors rose. Awful he rose,
And wan as the pale moon-beam o'er the tomb.
Still, as he mov'd, his form gigantic grew ;
Till pointing at the wretch's anguish'd heart
That dart which never errs, behold him breathe,
In wild despair, his last, yet curs'd with *sense* to feel
The dreadful visitations of his fate.

   Murder, at once the foulest and the first
Of human crimes, the eldest-born of sin,
In vain would hope its glowing guilt to hide
From the Omnipotent's all-piercing eye.
Whether in vale sequester'd darkly done,
Or on the summit of the mountain steep—
Whether conceal'd beneath the sea green wave,
Or left a corse disfigur'd on the shore,
Th' avenging spirit still shall call on heaven!
Ne'er can the trace of blood be wash'd away.
Or could the arid earth its steam imbibe,
Or could the deed of death be veil'd in night,
Yet the lost wretch whose hands have *once* been stain'd
Bears in his forehead the accusing mark.
The haggard cheek, the darkly-scowling eye,

The frenzied glance, the guilty, frequent start—
Ah! these are witnesses no wealth can bribe.
The slaves of *conscience* are they evermore,
And wearing all the livery of murder.

The four following Poems appeared, in the year 801, *in a Romance entitled " The Fatal Secret," and were written by me for the express purpose of being introduced in the course of that Work, to oblige the author. In the present publication they are more generalised.*

THE ORPHAN'S CURSE.

Ruin seize thee, ruthless man!
  Confusion on thy steps attend ;
Thy life exceed a mortal's span,
  And terror haunt thee to the end.

May every ill on man that pours
  Lurk in thy path, their stings to dart ;
Despair infest thy lonely hours,
  And drink the life-blood of thy heart!

If sleep thy wearied eyes should close,
  May dreams fantastic round thee rise,
And visions sad of future woes
  Disturb thee with their vengeful cries !

May poverty, disease, and care
  In swift succession seize their prey,
And mist and vapors blast the air
  That lights thy solitary way !

Without a friend to soothe thy care,
  Without a friend to close thine eyes,
To shades of darkness may'st thou go,
  And hell's fell monarch yield the prize !

Tremble ! for 'tis the orphan's pray'r,
  Nor hope to be forgiven :
The orphan's ghost thy soul shall scare,
  And bar the gates of heaven.

THE SKELETON PRIEST;

OR,

THE MARRIAGE OF DEATH.

The winds whistled loud the bleak caverns among,
The nightingale fearfully lower'd her song,
   The moon in dark vapors retir'd ;
When forth from her chamber, as midnight was told,
Irene descended, so fearless and bold—
   For love had her bosom inspir'd.

Her white veil it flutter'd as onward she flew,
Not regarding the tempest, tho' harsher it blew,
   Nor chill'd by the deep-piercing cold ;
The fire of passion that burn'd in her breast
All other emotions disdain'd and repress'd—
   For the power of love is untold.

Now sudden a flash that divided the skies,
And struck the lone maiden with awe and surprise,
    Illumin'd the desert around ;
She saw herself close to a precipice brink,
And as in mute horror she from it did shrink,
    " Beware !" cried a terrible sound.

" *Who* bids me beware?" she trembling exclaim'd ;
" Say, art thou a guardian who may not be nam'd,
    Or was it my fancy alone?"
Again she proceeded, determin'd to dare,
When slowly again cried the voice, " Oh, beware!"
    And sunk in a shudd'ring groan.

" What horror this night does Irene betide?
Orlando, my love, I shall ne'er be thy bride ;
    This night is the night of my doom.
Oh, spirit of darkness! wherever you be,
I ask but *this* night for my happiness free ;
    Let the *rest* be o'ershadow'd with gloom."

Once more she attempted the spot to depart;
She heard not the voice, and light grew her heart,
 No longer by terror subdu'd;
But scarce had she taken three steps of the way
When a lady, whose dress was more fair than the day,
 Of a sudden her footsteps pursu'd.

" O be not afraid, lovely maiden," she cried,
" But grant me the favor to walk by your side;
 My road is the same as your own:
The bride of Orlando you hasten to be,
But that is an hour you never may see,
 And 'tis gloomy to wander alone."

" Oh, prophet of woe!" said Irene, " forbear!"
And turn'd to the stranger with looks of despair,
 But enhorror'd withdrew from the sight:
A mouldering skull in her hand was display'd,
While a lamp the red blood on her bosom betray'd,
 And chequer'd the earth with its light.

" You start, lovely maiden ! What folly is fear !
And what in this skull can so hideous appear,
 Since you may resemble it soon ;
Unless you consent to be guided by me,
Return to your home, live contented and free,
 Or your journey *may end in the tomb*."

" No, never, while life in this bosom shall reign,
Will I treat my fond love with such cruel disdain,
 Or deny him my husband to be:
This night will I *wed* him, in despite of fate,
And fly with him, too, wheresoe'er he dictate,
 Whatever the sorrow to me."·

The stranger sigh'd deep as in autumn the wind ;
She turn'd her pale visage, so sad and resign'd,
 On Irene, and shuddering said,
" *Orlando is wedded.* This night, to be thine,
He committed on heaven and nature a crime
 Which in vengeance his soul must be paid.

" Still art thou resolv'd thy fond vice to pursue
In vain, for Orlando is hid from thy view,
  And wanders despairing alone:
His crime is his torment; by demons possess'd,
He gloomily wanders, depriv'd of his rest,
  In a desart by mountains o'ergrown.

" Then court not perdition; take homeward thy way,
Alone let *me* wander, alone let *me* stray,
  Or dread the reward of thy crime:
Forbear thou the union *cemented by blood,*
A *bond* of destruction to lure thee from good;
  The murderous compact resign.

" *Return,* and the past but a vision shall seem,
Appear on the morrow no more than a dream,
  Forgot in the glories of day:
Proceed, and before a short hour is told
Again, to your horror, you shall me behold,
  Your *blood as the forfeit to pay.*"

" Your name!" had Irene but faintly exclaim'd—
The stranger had vanish'd ; no traces remain'd ;
   The silence of *death* was around ;
The wind had subsided, the moon now appear'd,
Its beauteous refulgence the nightingale chear'd,
   And again did her harmony sound.

" Who dwells in this forest of gloom and despair?"
Cried Irene—" What horror impregnates the air?
   Do demons assemble to sport ?
They envy those raptures they cannot divide,
The rapture to be of Orlando the bride,
   And this is their infamous court.

" They mock at my feelings, they laugh at my pain,
But all their delusions they essay in vain—
   Orlando, *I still will be thine!*"
Then onward she sprang. At the foot of the hill
Orlando impatiently waited her still,
   And their arms in fond rapture entwine.

But the arms of Orlando than ice were more cold,
As in them Irene he seem'd to enfold ;

His features were hid from her view ;
His voice seemed hollow, he mournfully sigh'd;
A chilling despondence crept over the bride,

A mistrust that she dar'd not pursue.

" Orlando, what demons have lurk'd in my way
Thine Irene from all that she lov'd to delay,

And say thou wert wedded from me?"
" No more, fair Irene !   The hour is right ;
" I little expected thy presence to-night :

Our wedding shall speedily be.

" Behind this green hill, just close to the beach,
Is a vessel in which our castle we reach,

Now gloomy, and anxious for *you.*
Come, quickly depart—time onward does fly ;
Since here you have ventur'd you must not deny."

And forward Irene he drew.

Now approaching the beach, lo! a vessel was there;
Of mist seem'd the cables, the sails vapors fair,
   No creature to guide it was nigh;
Orlando took charge of his terrified bride,
It seem'd like an arrow the waves to divide,
   And swifter than fancy to fly.

Now reaching the opposite shore, he convey'd
From the vessel of shadows the heart-frozen maid,
   When instant it faded from view:
He forc'd her still on through a rocky descent,
Her feet and her bosom were cruelly rent,
   And blood did each footstep pursue.

They enter'd a cavern; an altar was there;
A priest to unite them does slowly prepare;
   Their hands are together entwin'd;
When *casting* his robe, lo! what horrors beneath!
The *skeleton priest* was no other than *Death*,
   Whom the maiden in marriage had join'd.

" Thou art wedded, but *not to Orlando*—behold!

For, maiden, thy love was imprudent and bold—

    Thou art wedded, and must to *my* home.

Orlando no longer—dissolv'd is the spell ;

Thy nuptial rejoicing must be a death knell,

    For thou art the *wife of the tomb*.

Irene, despairing, remember'd the wood—

Before her the spectre now menacing stood—

    " The wife of Orlando was *I;*

He sent my soul wand'ring, thy beauties to gain ;

I warn'd thee, alas! but I warn'd thee in vain,

    For *thou* wert determin'd to die."

Alas! sad Irene no more can depart ;

The numbness of death slowly crept round her heart,

    And, palsied, her nerves seem'd to shrink :

The *skeleton priest* now approach'd them again ;

He seiz'd on the victim—her struggles were vain—

    From the world, lo, together they sink!

JULIA'S MURDER;

OR,

THE SONG OF WOE.

What hast thou done, oh! wretch despairing?
　　Think with horror on thy crime;
Deep remorse, thy bosom tearing,
　　Ne'er must hope a balm from time.
Julia sweet! who could alarm her?
Fiends of hell could only harm her,

　　　　　　　　　　Lovely flow'r.

Ev'ry gale that wafts around thee
　　Shall Altona " murd'ress" call;
Ev'ry whisper shall confound thee,
　　Ev'ry shadow shall appall.
Terror evermore pursue thee!
Guilt itself shall blush to view thee,

　　　　　　　　　　Murd'ress dire!

Julia's ghost shall rise to scare thee,
  Sighing in the hollow wind,
" Cruel sister, oh! beware thee—
  Swift destruction shalt thou find."
Hope flies aghast whilst thou art here ;
The sun forgets its power to chear,
                  Accurs'd of heaven !

Thy breath empoisons the sweet air ;
  Where'er thou step'st a blight is found ;
Thine eyes the *birds of Heaven scare*—
  Thou spread'st a pestilence around.
When thy with'ring breath is flown,
What hand so rash to place thy stone,
                  Disgrace of hell ?

The fragrant earth would ne'er receive thee,
  Disease would rise to blast mankind;
E'en ocean's waves alarm'd would leave thee,
  And fearful o'er thee rush the wind.
For deeds of horror wert thou born,
To laugh all human guilt to scorn,
                  And curse the world.

Sin, rising from her cavern dark,
  Shrinks appal'd, and howling flies,
And, trembling thy crimes to mark,
  E'en palsied Horror shudd'ring dies.
Where'er thou art, despair is ours ;
Shrunk and wither'd are the pow'rs

  Of nature now.

Let this earth sink, and chaos come,
  A *new* and *spotless* world arise,
For ages ne'er can steep in gloom
  The guilt that for *oblivion* cries.
No time thy deed can fade away,
Its memory blasts the coming day,

  And threats perdition.

THE AIREAL CHORUS;

OR,

THE WARNING.

" Lady, whither would you stray?
  Tempt no more this dang'rous wood;
Blood-besprinkled is the way,
  Evil lurks, to injure good.

" Lady, home, and swiftly, go;
  Horror follows as you fly:
Lady, wherefore linger so?
  Hasten, or prepare to die.

" I was once a virgin fair,
  Morven lov'd, and thought him true;
Morven left me to despair—
  Morven thus will do by you.

" Lady, then no more delay ;
  Hear me *warn*—in haste depart:
Fiends, assembling in your way,
  Long to feast upon your heart.

" Round a cauldron—round and round,
  Lo! they brew a horrid charm ;
Magic words, of direful sound,
  Shall your pow'rs of flight disarm.

" Fly, oh! fly this dusky wood,
  O'er the flame your fibres shrink ;
Drunk, they riot on your blood,
  Reeling, tott'ring as they drink.

" Lo! they thirst, they rage for you,
  Yelling hoarse with fearful cry ;
Wild with transport they pursue,
  Laughing loud to see you fly.

" Vain your flight—I sadly tell
  Hope of mercy too is vain ;
If you step in magic spell,
  Never may you turn again.

"Lo! they rush—they seize you now—
  In your bosom dart their fangs;
Now your blood begins to flow—
  Wild they suck amid your pangs.

"Spent with fury, now give o'er—
  Yelling bear you swift away;
Sink to hell, and rise no more
  Till they scent another prey.

"I was once a virgin fair,
  Morven lov'd, and thought him true;
Morven left me to despair—
  Morven thus will do by you.

"Lady, then no more delay;
  Hear me *warn*—in haste depart:
Fiends, assembling in your way,
  Long to feast upon your heart."

DEATH AND THE LADY.

In imitation of the old English ballads.

DEATH.

Lady, lady, come with me,
  I am thy true friend;
New and strange sights shalt thou see
  If thine hand thou'lt lend.

LADY.

Wo is me, what dost thou here?
  Spectre foul, away!
No more let me those accents hear
  Which fill me with dismay.

DEATH.

Thou shalt lie in my arms to-night;
  My bed is narrow and cold;
When morning dawns there is no light,
  For its curtains are made of *mould*.

LADY.

Ah, me! ah, me! what's that you say?
  And what the bed you mean?
Ah! if I dream, God send it day,
  And drive you from mine eyne!

DEATH.

Lady, lady, it must not be;
  Look on me once again;
In different shapes you oft see me,
  The friend of grief and pain.

LADY.

Oh! sure I once have look'd on thee,
  Thy vest is snowy white;
Tall is thy form, I did it see
  By yonder pale moonlight.

The mortal lay in a silken bed
    Of bright and gaudy hue,
On a pillow of down repos'd her head,
    Bound with a fillet of blue.

The tall sprite now her bed drew near,
    And stretch'd the curtains wide ;
The mortal glanc'd in trembling fear,
    But swift her face did hide.

For his robe of mist no more conceal'd
    His skeleton form from view,
Each white rib was to sight reveal'd,
    And his eyeless sockets too.

Tall and lank, and sadly gaunt,
    His rueful form was seen,
His grisly ribs no flesh could vaunt,
    Misty the space between.

———

DEATH.

Lady, fresh and fair there are,
   Young and blooming too;
Fate, nor fresh nor young will spare,
   Nor now can favour you.

LADY.

Not in my prime?   Oh! say not so;
   Fair the morn will be,
Gaily rise when I am low,
   The sun no more to see.

DEATH.

Hast thou not seen the sun, I pray,
   Full many a time before?
Hast thou not curs'd the tardy day,
   And wept till it was o'er?

LADY.

Alas! I thought not what I said:
   Oh, Death, in pity spare!
Let me not with thee be laid
   While I am young and fair.

DEATH.

What hast thou known but care and sorrow ?
  Thy lovers faithless all ?
And if I spare thee till to-morrow
  Some horrid ill may fall.

LADY.

'Tis true no peace I've ever known,
  My days have pass'd in woe ;
I trust, since those in grief have gone,
  The rest will not thus go.

DEATH.

Deceitful hope ! to-morrow's dawn
  A dire mishap shall bring ;
From my dim shades I come to warn—
  Thy *friend* as well as King.

LADY.

Ah, yet awhile, ah, yet awhile,
  This ill I do not fear ;
By care I may its course beguile,
  But why com'st *thou* so near ?

DEATH.

Mortal wretched, mortal vain!
　　Child of weakest woe!
Sickness, sorrow, tears, and pain
　　Are all you e'er can know.

Say, what in *life* is there to lure
　　Thy agitated mind?
Trifling, futile, vain, unsure—
　　Oh, wherefore art thou blind?

Thou dost not live e'en *half* thy day,
　　For part is spent in tears;
In sleep how much is worn away!
　　How much in hopes and fears!

In doubt you move, in doubt you live,
　　Surrounded by a cloud;
Nor up can pierce, nor downward dive,
　　And yet of *life* are proud.

Danger, danger lurks around,
　　False is the smile of man;
Unsteady is the sinking ground,
　　Delusions croud thy span.

Is there a bliss you e'er can feel
　　Your million woes to pay?
Is there a day which fails to steal
　　Some transient joy away?

Is there a beam, which gilds thy morn
　　With radiance falsely bright,
That sinks not in the evening storm
　　Which crushes thee ere night?

Life is a bitter, bitter hour,
　　A bleak, a dreary wild,
Where blooms no shrub, where blows no flow'r
　　For nature's wretched child.

If from the grave to look on life
　　With retrospective eye
We sad could view its noisy strife,
　　Who would not wish to die?

A fev'rish dream, a bubble frail,
　　Borne on inconstant air.
The bubble bursts—there's none bewail,
　　For thousands *still* are there!

No trace remains—the world goes on
   As tho' *thou* ne'er hadst been ;
Thou griev'st to die, others grieve none,
   Nor miss thee from the scene.

A speck in nature's vast profound,
   Unknown thy life or birth—
Giddily flying in the round,
   Then add a grain to earth.

Mortal wretched, mortal vain,
   Longer wilt thou stay ?
Longer wilt thou suffer pain,
   Or cheat the coming day ?

———

And then the spectre heav'd a sigh,
   A sigh both long and deep,
In mist his changeful form drew nigh,
   And he saw the mortal weep.

Then far, far off 'twas seen to glide,
   Shrouded in vapours blue ;
Small, small it seem'd, but did not hide,
   Then gradual rose to view.

With dazzling light the chamber shone,
    And tall the sprite appear'd,
And when the solemn bell toll'd one,
    The lady no longer fear'd.

" Come quit thy bed, fair lady, I say,
    For mine, which is narrow and cold;
When morning dawns there is no day,
    For its curtains are made of mould.

" But I'll give thee a robe of vapors blue,
    Nor laces nor silks have I;
I'll gem thy brows with a fillet of dew,
    Which lasts *but while you die.*

" And I'll give you to her from whom you came,
    Your bed shall be peaceful and lone;
Your mother's cold arms will embrace you again,
    And your covering shall be stone.

" There no more griefs shall ever you know,
    Nor day nor night shall you see;
Secure in your narrow bed below,
    Companion true to me."

" God pardon me," the lady cried,

  " And receive me to thy feet,

And all that pure and holy died,

  Oh ! grant that I may meet."

Then rising from her silken bed,

  She gave her hand to Death ;

His touch'd, benumb'd, her soul with dread,

  And stopp'd her rising breath.

THE ELFIN KING;

OR,

THE SCOFFER PUNISHED.

After the manner of some modern Poets.

As I cross'd the desert wild,
  Not a star amid the gloom,
Loud and harsh the tempest howl'd,
  Driving vapours o'er the moon.

What care I for tempest loud?
  What care I for desert lone?
What care I for church-yard blank,
  Or spectre flitting round its tomb?

For white-rob'd phantom, elf, or gnome
    What care I, both brave and free?
Then howl, rude tempest, till thou burst,
    All thy howling moves not me.

So sang I careless, " Wo to me!"
    When, lo, a distant light appear'd;
Methought the village near must be,
    And joy soon my bosom chear'd.

" Stop!" a voice shriek'd most shrill;
    Close to my ear the sound did seem,
While o'er my cheek a freezing breath
    Rush'd cold as tho' it death had been.

" What now," I cried, " unmanner'd lout?
    Shew thyself, and tell thy mind."
" *Mind!*" the voice shriek'd amain,
    And now it sounded from behind.

Close to my side a light I see,
    In cloven hoof, of grinning spite;
My soul grew sick, and back I drew,
    Possess'd with wonder and affright.

Large his head, as cauldron round,
   Slight his waist, as sea-weed thin,
With face behind and face before,
   And reaching to his feet each chin.

Cover'd o'er with hair so white,
   Drest in robe of dusky blue;
Where eyes should be two imps look'd out,
   Glaring hideous to the view.

On each shoulder sat a bird,
   Its plumage was of fiery red,
Transparent, bright, you through them saw,
   And with their beaks they peck'd his head.

Teeth he had, both long and green,
   Seeming slim'd with sea-weed o'er,
And, crawling slow his legs between,
   A mastiff huge, with tail before.

Feet nor hands this elfin had,
   But hoofs instead so black had he;
His putrid breath made blisters rise,
   Tho' cold as any ice might be.

Loudly laugh'd the elfin sprite,
  Closely clinging round my knee,
And in his hoof a rattle turn'd,
  Which, in good truth, near deafen'd me.

Sinking to the earth was I,
  When, lo! a vision, tall and thin,
Pluck'd my arm, and taunting cried,
  " Good sir, how brave do you begin !"

Stiff as marble did she bend,
  Like a steeple tall, I vow ;
Where her head lodg'd---that, in faith,
  Was more than ever I could know.

Thin her form as fairy wand,
  White as snow of dazz'ling hue,
Her fingers swept the dusky ground,
  She zigzag danc'd before my view.

Holding up her misty train,
  An hideous fury crept behind,
With horse's head, and fish's tail,
  And body of a feather'd kind.

Near her came a small black man,
  With fiery sparks all studded o'er;
Now he swam on air, and yell'd,
  And coolly then trudg'd on before.

Long and crooked was his nose,
  Curling underneath his chin,
Red his eyes as harvest suns,
  With a copper horn between.

Little imps with fiery eyes,
  Serpents which, if cut in twain,
For a moment vanish'd back,
  Then, multiplied, return'd again.

Animals with human face,
  Cats with plumage of a bird,
Sprites that hideous did grimace,
  But scorn'd to say a single word.

Goblins dancing in the air
  With curious gambols you might see,
Arms and legs that mov'd alone,
  And things as strange as well might be.

Horror stiffen'd ev'ry nerve ;
    " Save me, save me !" loud I cry :
Swift my hair is twisted round,
    Sudden I am borne on high,

" Learn to sport with elfin king,"
    A voice so shrill assail'd my ear :
I seem'd to wake—but, oh ! dismay !
    On precipice I lay most near.

Slowly, cautiously, I roll
    From the dashing torrent's roar,
Which, foaming in the rocky cave,
    Had near embrac'd me evermore.

Oh ! woe was me ! full twenty mile
    Astray the elfins had me ta'en.
I wander'd home, and vow'd the while
    I ne'er with elfs would sport again.

SIMILE.

THE little Moth round candle turning,
Stops not till its wings are burning :
So woman, dazzled by man's wooing,
Rushes to her own undoing.

FRACAS BETWEEN THE DEITIES.

ADDRESSED TO MR. F——, AN ENTHUSIASTIC VOTARY
AT THE SHRINE OF BACCHUS.

(Written at sixteen.)

ROSY Bacchus and Pallas once had an affray,
　　Where neither would precedence yield;
For each seem'd determin'd on gaining the day,
　　And routing the foe from the field.

Says Bacchus, " You'll grant, me most mortals adore,
　　And with rapture resort to my court;
While for *you* only greybeards and dotards explore,
　　When age has forbid them to sport."

H 2

Says Pallas, " You're right;" and she bow'd on her
    shield :
  " This indeed is the first of your hits ;
For e'er since my father his sceptre could wield,
    The *fools* have outnumber'd the *wits*."

An emotion of rage fill'd young Bacchus's breast ;
    And snatching some grapes from his brow,
Disdainful he threw them at Pallas's crest,
    While his ruby cheeks redder did grow.

" Nay now, trust me," says Pallas, " I meant no
    offence ;
    But you know, my dear Bacchus, *I* came
From the forehead of Jove when he smote it for sense,
    My conquest should give you no shame."

" Now Pluto swift drag me o'er Styx to his hell,
    And bid water be ever my drink,
If e'er, owlish goddess, I yield thee the bell,
    Or Bacchus at woman shall shrink.

" What avail *your* tough maxims and mischievous
>lore,
>But to render men crafty, or sad ?
>Nor even to lighten the wond'rous bore,
>Is a drop of *my* juice to be had."

" Ah, poor little baby !" cried Pallas again ;
>" Let thy vine cover'd pate be at rest :
>To wage war with *Wisdom*, young Toper, is vain,
>You'll only come off *second best*."

As thus they disputed, Love, bounding along,
>Chanc'd together his messmates to see ;
>And sportively bowing, he cried, " Am I wrong,
>Or do Bacchus and Pallas agree?"

" Ah, Cupid, how fare you ?—come hither, my boy,"
>Says Pallas ;—" but first, I beseech,
>Put your bows in their quiver;—your present employ
>Is to *heal*, not occasion a breach.

н 3

" Little Bacchus, poor imp there, has offer'd to
   prove
  His pow'r as superior to mine,
As thine, pretty torturer, exquisite Love,
  Is superior to him and his wine."

" Will Love from the cause of his *pleader* depart ?"
  Cried Bacchus—and angrily star'd ;
" His chief *aid-de-camp*, who seduces the heart,
  Already for rapture prepar'd."

" Hush awhile, mighty wranglers (cried Cupid) I pray,
  Or, by Venus! I sheer off the stage ;
I protest I'm quite scar'd by this hideous affray,
  And my nerves are unstrung for an age.

" Now mark *my* decision impartial and plain,
  Both are mighty in different ways ;
And neither infringing the other's domain,
  May command equal tribute of praise.

" You, beauteous Minerva, too closely pursued,
　　Will harass and torture the mind;
While Bacchus, with tempting allurements endued,
　　Is often *destructively* kind.

" The flowers of knowledge lead mortals astray,
　　To grasp them they forfeit their ease;
And, Bacchus, *thy* votaries, stupidly gay,
　　See not poison conceal'd in thy lees.

" Then to steer clear of madness, and pale melancholy,
　　I will strew my gay roses between;
Each in turn shall be sued, without sadness or folly,
　　And *Love* shall embellish the scene."

LOGAN'S GRAVE.

LONE in the desart rose his peaceful tomb;
  No sorrowing friend at morn or eve pass'd by;
But when a pitying moon-beam chas'd the gloom,
  Forth came his spirit sad, and linger'd nigh.

RUIN'D INNOCENCE,

Written at seventeen,

UPON THE SAME OCCASION AS " THE EXILE."

SEE'ST thou yon lily in its blooming pride,
  Its snowy bosom op'ning to the view,
  Surcharg'd with gems of bright and fragrant dew,
With envy view'd by ev'ry flow'r beside ?

'Tis the fair idol of the gard'ner's toil,
  Rais'd by his hand, the fav'rite of the vale,
  Kiss'd by the sun, and courted by the gale,
Confess'd the glory of the lovely soil.

Too happy sweet !—for now the pirate hand
  Longs to purloin thee from thy native bed ;
  Prefers thou should'st be *his,* and shortly dead,
Than gaily bloom amid thy spotless band.

A moment snaps thy halcyon life in twain,
    Some selfish wight, devoid of soul, decrees
    That thou should'st *die* his vacant mind to please,
And then, despoil'd, be cast abroad again.

Cast, haply, on the spot where lately too
    In beauty's pride thou little dreamt thy fate;
    Despis'd by those who envied thee so late,
And crush'd by feet that once were stopp'd to view.

The gard'ner who thy charms was wont to greet,
    Missing thy beauty from the fragrant bow'r,
    Bestows his care upon some gaudier flow'r,
And *knows* thee not—disfigur'd at his feet.

So the bright vestal, 'mid the circle gay,
    Awhile is gaz'd at, envied, and admir'd;
    Then by the fell destroyer, *man*, desir'd,
Obtain'd—and *then*—unpitied cast away.

Now sidelong view'd by wretches vulgar born;
    Sneer'd at, or *pitied*, by the mock refin'd;—
    Pity, degrading to the feeling mind,
And bitterer than of ignorance the *scorn*.

Despis'd—dishonor'd—driv'n forth alone ;
   What stone, unconscious, rests her patient head ?
   Or sod ungenial, yields that breast a bed,
Where happy innocence once held her throne !

Or list'ning to the next seducer's tale,
   Has she awhile her gloomy fate delay'd ?
   In vain—it follows like a vengeful shade,
And tho' now distant—hope not it shall fail.

Glitter awhile the pageant of the hour,
   Bright as the gem that glistens on the thorn,
   More short-liv'd even than the fleeting morn,
Drank in the ray which lent its faithless pow'r.

Affect the mirth thy languid soul disdains,
   Laugh while false rapture lightens from thine eye ;
   The transitory *smile* shall haste to die,
While melancholy still its place maintains.

Prophetic of the fate that, nurs'd in gloom,
   Lingers to strike at thy devoted breast,
   A victim to the crimes of man confest,
And drives thee thro' destruction to the tomb.

MOORISH COMBAT.

THE breeze was hush'd; the modest moon-beam slept
  On the green bosom of the treach'rous wave ;
The lover Marli wander'd forth alone,
  And trembling linger'd near the well-known cave.

A snow-white turban crown'd his brow severe,
  Its crescent sparkled like the beamy morn ;
A dazzling vest his graceful form array'd,
  And gems unnumber'd did his belt adorn.

" Come, lovely Ora, pure as angels are,
  Light as yon clouds that o'er the moon now sail ;
And let thy beauteous form like hers appear,
  Refulgent, thro' the dim night's dusky veil.

Come, gentle as the mild refreshing dew
  Upon th' enamour'd bosom of the rose;
Come thou, and calm my eager thirsty soul,
  And like the dew upon my breast repose.

Come, Paradise of sweets ! thy fragrant love
  Shall steal through ev'ry fibre of my brain ;
Thy sight shall seem unto my fever'd sense,
  As doth to desart sands the pitying rain."

He said—when sudden from the cavern dark,
  Like a fair sprite soft issuing from the tomb,
An angel form was slowly seen to rise,
  And trembling pause, as doubtful of her doom.

" My Ora's form !" the panting youth exclaim'd,
  And eager clasp'd her to his love-sick breast;
Wild throbb'd his heart, and from his sparkling eyes
  The fire of love shot quick, as Ora prest.

Say, did they rest between each fervent kiss ?
  Ah! no; but while their flutt'ring sighs unite,
No moisture e'er their glowing lips might cool,
  Swiftly dried up by passion's fierce delight.

How vain to stem their rapture as it flow'd,
　Or whisper to their stagg'ring sense, beware!
His eyes inebriate wander'd o'er her charms,
　While hers to earth were cast with chastened air.

Lo! from a mountain's steep and shadowy side,
　O'er which obliquely yet the beams were thrown,
The fierce Zampogni, vengeance in his eye,
　Shot like a flaming meteor swiftly down.

And now he paus'd, and scowling fell around,
　His arm uplifted, and his breath restrain'd,
The flow'rs and herbage wither'd in his gaze,
　While he from instant vengeance scarce refrain'd.

Not long on thoughts of horror did he pause—
　Bright as the beam that gilds the ev'ning cloud,
His sparkling sabre swift divides the pair,
　And seeks in either breast a crimson shroud.

But wrath intemp'rate ne'er can justly aim.—
　For deeds of valour as for love renown'd,
The gallant Marli drew his keen-edg'd blade,
　And fierce Zampogni bit the dusty ground.

Yet swift he rose, and urg'd the dubious fight;
  Such warriors sure before had ne'er engag'd;
While victory alternate promis'd each
    The lovely prize for whom the battle rag'd.

She, beauteous maid! like a bright genius stood,
  With hands and eyes uplifted to the sky;
While steely sparks commingling with the beam,
    Were not more bright than shot from either eye.

But now a thrust with vengeful fury giv'n,
  Flush'd in Zampogni's cheek the hopeful blood;
Mysterious fate directs the flying steel—
    Ah, Marli! thou hast ne'er the stroke withstood.

On Ora, see, his dying eyes are cast—
  " Thou art Zampogni's now," he faintly said;
" Yet, sunshine of my soul—ah! let me gaze
    Upon those charms which from before me fade."

" Yes, thou art *mine*," the fierce Zampogni cried;
  And to the maid advanc'd with frantic air.
" Rather the Grave's," indignant Ora cried.—
    " Die, traitor! and avenge my love's despair."

A dagger, in her vest till now conceal'd,
　　She buried in the gloomy rival's breast.
He fell, in death majestic—withering rage
　　And stern contempt his features *still* exprest.

" And thou, Oh, Marli! thou for whom alone
　　The wretched Ora liv'd—thou *yet* art mine;
Then thus with reeking steel our *vow* I bind,
　　In death as life, oh, Marli! only thine."

THE MANIAC *.

WILD thro' the desert woods Alzira flew !
    Her robe disorder'd hung ;
Wet were her locks from midnight's chilly dew,
    Her snowy arms were bare ;
    Her bosom fair
    With blood was stain'd ;
But reckless still the lovely wretch remain'd,
    As dolefully she sung—

* This poem was originally set to music in its present state, but making too many variations necessary, it was retrenched, and altered to the form in which it is now published for the piano forte.

" Ye idle gales that play around me,
 Waft a whisper to my love,
 He resides somewhere above;
 Say to meet him I will fly
 Soon as I have leave to die;
E'en now death's harbingers surround me;
 Tell him so, and take him this;"
 She said, and gave the winds a kiss.

Then started madly from her earthy bed,
Her nerves were fever'd, and convuls'd her brow;
 Her unsettled eye
 Wander'd high, then low
  Alternately——
 The pow'r of thought had fled.
Eager she gain'd the mountain's slippery top,
 Her bosom bare and bleeding,
When, lo! soft strains delay'd her wild proceeding,
 And sudden made her stop.

Her lover was return'd; his voice well known
 Struck thro' her madden'd brain
  Its tone——

Then swift again
Her short remembrance flies,
Like light'ning darting o'er the gloomy plain,
Flashes and dies!

Just then the hurrying moon broke from a cloud,
Although the angry winds blew loud,
To shew the lover where his mistress stood,
Seeming on death with haggard air to brood.
He mark'd her dang'rous state,
And fear'd he ne'er could save;
Sigh'd, lest her dreadful fate
Should be an instant grave—

" Oh, stop!" he cried,
And saw her eye-balls glaring wide,
Of bright and dazzling blue;
Uncertain trod her dubious feet,
The lover's heart with terror beat—
Aghast he stood, tortur'd with keen alarms;
She flew——
He caught her in his trembling arms!

His burning tears fell on her woe-worn face,

    With painful joy he clasp'd her to his breast;

Her shrunk heart flutter'd in the dear embrace.

    Still fell his tears as closer still he prest;

And as the dew revives a drooping flow'r,

She rais'd her head, and testified their pow'r !

THE POOR NEGRO SADI.

AH ! poor negro Sadi, what sorrows, what anguish
  Oppress the lone victim fate dooms for a slave !
What eye or what heart o'er those sorrows shall lan-
      guish ?
  What finger point out the lone African's grave ?

First torn like a wretch from his innocent dwelling,
  And torn from Abouka, the wife of his soul,
Then forc'd, while his heart was indignantly swelling,
  To bow his proud neck to the despot's controul.

Think not, European, tho' dark his complexion,
  Dark, dark as the hue of the African's fate,
That his *mind* is devoid of the light of reflexion,
  And knows not distinctions of love or of hate.

And believe, when you see him in agony bending
 Beneath the hard lash, if he fainting should pause,
That pure are to heaven his sorrows ascending,
 And dear must you pay for the torture you cause.

Mark, mark the red blood that, so eloquent streaming,
 Appeals to the Godhead thou sayest is thine!
Mark, mark the sunk eye that on heaven is beaming!
 It calls deep revenge on *oppression* and *crime*.

The poor negro Sadi—what horror befel him,
 To slavery dragg'd in the bloom of his years!
To the food he disdains the vile lash must compel
   him,
 Ah! food doubly bitter when moisten'd by tears!

At length, in a moment of anguish despairing,
 Poor Sadi resolves to escape, or he dies :
He plung'd in the ocean, not knowing nor caring
 If e'er from its waves he was doom'd to arise.

He skims light as down, when at distance espying
   A vessel, its refuge he struggles to gain ;
And nearly exhausted, just sinking, just dying,
   Escapes from a grave in the pitiless main.

But vainly preserv'd, sable victim of sorrow !
   An end far more dreadful thine anguish must have ;
Tho' a moment from hope it faint lustre may borrow,
   Soon, soon must it sink in the gloom of the grave.

Soft, soft blew the gale, and the green billows swell-
      ing,
   Gay sail'd the light vessel for Albion's shore ;
Poor Sadi sigh'd deep for his wife and his dwelling,
   That wife and that dwelling he ne'er must see more.

Oh, Britons ! so fam'd in the annals of glory,
   The poor negro Sadi is cast on your plains—
Oh, Britons ! if just be your fame or your glory,
   The poor negro Sadi shall bless your domains.

As yet see he wanders forlorn and in sadness,
  By many scarce seen, and unpitied by all;
No glance yet his sunk heart has flutter'd with gladness,
  Nor voice sympathetic on him seem'd to call.

In vain, wretched negro! thou lookest around thee—
  In vain, wretched negro! so lowly dost bend;
Tho' a thousand cold faces for ever surround thee,
  Among them not one is, poor Sadi, thy friend.

Three nights and three days had he wander'd despairing,
  No food nor no shelter the victim had found;
The pangs of keen hunger his bosom were tearing,
  When, o'erpower'd with torture, he sunk on the
    ground.

He clasp'd his thin hands, now no longer imploring
  The succour which all had so basely denied,
In hopeless submission had finish'd deploring
  The suff'rings he felt must so shortly subside.

On the step of a door his faint body reclining
    Had sought unmolested to yield up its breath,
But hell-born tormentors forbade his resigning
    Within their vile precincts, his sorrows to death.

They dragg'd the lone victim, in misery lying,
    From off the cold stone where he languish'd to rest,
Defenceless they dragg'd him, unpitied—tho' dying,
    His last wretched moments with horror opprest!

Now keen blew the tempest, and keener still blowing,
    His shrunk heart scarce flutter'd, scarce heav'd his
        faint breath—
His blood was congeal'd, and his tears no more flowing,
    Had froze on his eyelids, now closing in death.

Oh, Heaven! that seest this sad wretch expiring
    By famine's keen tortures, unaided, alone,
Pure, pure to *thy* throne his last sighs are aspiring,
    Tho' sable his skin, tho' *unchristian* his tone!

Oh, poor negro Sadi! what sorrows, what anguish .

  Oppress the lone victim fate dooms for a slave!

What eye or what heart for those sorrows shall lan-
     guish?

  What finger point out the lone African's grave?

THE DYING LOVER.

*Written for a friend, whose lover, an amiable young
man, died the martyr of a swift decline.*

OH, lovely youth! why seem thy cheeks so pale?
  Oh, lovely youth! why are thine eyes so hollow?
Oh, live! or, rather than thy loss bewail,
  To the cold grave thy lifeless corse I'd follow.

So spoke I to the idol of my love,
  While in my heart I felt a deadly sorrow;
As with slow steps he languidly did move,
  I thought with dreadful doubt upon the morrow.

The morrow came, and yet my lover liv'd;
  Against a tree I saw his form reclining:
To heaven, with such a look my heart as riv'd,
  He cast his eyes, with pious sweetness shining.

Ah! yes, toward the glorious sun he gaz'd
  With languid smile, that said adieu for ever,
And patiently his wasted hands he rais'd,
  Ah, fatal morn! forget it shall I never!

In brighter beauty, too, than morn he smil'd,
  On his white cheek the red rose gaily blooming,
A momentary hope my soul beguil'd,
  Which fate to deeper agony was dooming.

Oh, cruel malady! like some false friend
  The livery of truth and kindness wearing,
Remorseless can the heart with daggers rend,
  Which, trusting in thy smiles, is left despairing.

Now sank the joyous sun-beams in the west,
  O'er his thin form a transient brightness casting;
The lovely wretch that they so gaily dress'd
  Scarce than that transient brightness seem'd more
     lasting!

But, like th' anemony, most frail and fair,

   With the last beam his fainting form expiring,

His spotless soul escap'd this world of care,

   And seem'd, methought, upon that beam retiring !

From that sad hour no peace can I e'er know,

   An early blight my fondest hopes destroying ;

For tho' in spring frail flowers again may blow,

   No second spring is there for my enjoying.

THE SOVEREIGNTY OF LOVE.

AH, mock not me! for *you* have never lov'd,
Nor have you e'er, like me, its sorrows prov'd,
Nor have you e'er, like me, its pleasures tasted;
In languid medium all your life has wasted.
No transport wild your soul has ever fir'd,
Whether by bliss or agony inspir'd;
No swift transition from despair to joy
Did e'er your soul's harmonic tones destroy;
No fever'd passion that, like mine, has burn'd,
The even current of your blood e'er turn'd :
Listless and cool each sober hour has pass'd,
While mine in feeling various have been cast.

O! I have lov'd to such a mad excess,
No thought can reach, nor any words express :

Refining on my love, I so have stray'd,
Fancy has languish'd on the rack she made!
How oft the solitary shade I've sought,
To brood with pleasure o'er my own fond thought!
Reason has stagger'd on her trembling throne,
And wild imagination reign'd alone.
Beyond this earth my soaring hopes aspire;
Death SHALL not quench true passion's sacred fire!
Ethereal essence from the grave shall rise,
And *conscious* souls claim kindred in the skies!

Oh, Memory! well I with thine aid can trace
My hero's beauty and his manly grace.
How oft his bosom hath my pillow been!
How oft repress'd the starting tear I've seen,
When sad remembrance would his smile destroy,
And thoughts of absence blast his rising joy!
I lov'd him! yes, my throbbing heart well knows,
And, conscious, with increas'd emotion glows—
Yes, with keen ardour have I fondly lov'd—
Dearly my truth and passion have I prov'd;
No future hope, no joy have thought so great,
That on Love's shrine I would not immolate.

Yet, in return, I mistress sole would be,
No joy, no hope, but must depend on me ;
My frown must sink, my smile must elevate,
My wish be law, and my command be fate.
I ev'ry sense, I ev'ry nerve must sway,
And, only touch'd by me, each passion play :
No *second* object must have power to move—
I suffer no competitor in love;
But, like the polar star in gloomy night,
Must lead alone, by my superior light.

Such my desire! nor less contents my soul,
And such I *once* possess'd, in gay controul.
No madd'ning jealousy! no doubts, no fears,
No weak complaining, nor no woman's tears,
No mild reproaches, no degrading grief!
E'er pain'd, then left *my* soul without relief;
I felt pre-eminent, my power I knew,
And from that knowledge all my passion grew.

Could I then think upon a newer lover?
Or waste a thought upon some wand'ring rover

No—solitary, sad my life shall fade,

No languid pref'rence e'er my heart invade.

Retiring, scornful, sceptical, unblest,

No *second* love my *first* shall ever wrest;

Depriv'd of him, his memory shall retain

The *fond, proud* heart he *only* knew to gain.

TO THE SHADE OF MARY ROBINSON.

HOW sadly, sweet seraph, I mourn that I never,
 I ne'er was so happy thee living to know!
How sadly I mourn that the time is gone ever!
 And the wish of my bosom must end in vain woe.

How sadly I mourn, lovely seraph, while thinking
 That now, in the cold gloomy night of the tomb,
Thou know'st not one heart for thy sorrows is sinking,
 One heart that bemoans, with regret, thy sad doom.

How oft, too, I mourn that an heart form'd to love
  thee—
 An heart which responsive had beat to thine own,
Can from thy cell narrow now never remove thee,
 Where tranquil thou liest, unconscious and lone.

Oh, world, cruel world! how I shrink, how I tremble
   An angel so gracious should be so forlorn!
Oh, world, cruel world! there is none that resemble,
   Among you, an angel like her that is gone.

Like a cedar amid the rude desart high soaring,
   And looking contempt on the shrubs that surround,
Enduring for years the tempest loud roaring,
   And scorning to yield until *broke to the ground.*

Ah! then, with what joy, ye shrubs so presuming,
   Ye rustle and wave o'er the cedar's *proud* grave!
But degrading your safety, and mean your assuming,
   Adversity's storm only buffets the brave!

Oh, thou! whose high virtues, angelic, yet glorious,
   At once move my wonder, my pride, and my tears,
Still, still in the grave dost thou triumph victorious,
   Thy fame sounding loud in thine *enemies'* ears!

The wretches, who envied, who fear'd thy perfection,
   O'er the threshold of life drove thee trembling away,
Shall yet shudder and sicken, when harass'd reflexion
   O'erwhelms with remorse the retributive day.

Oh! say, from thy cold, narrow bed, lovely Mary,
　　Say, couldst thou not wander, to smile upon me?
Oh! why not, sometimes, in thy form light and airy,
　　Deign in the deep wild my companion to be?

Oh! why not, sometimes, when I wander in sadness,
　　Glide distant before me—seen dim thro' the trees?
Or how would my heart bound with mystical gladness
　　If thy *voice* were heard, sounding sweet in the breeze!

Or why not, o'ershadow'd by yon drooping willow,
　　At eve let me mark thee reclining beneath?
Or by moonlight upborne, on the edge of the billow,
　　Fantastic, and light as of zephyr the breath?

Ah! around thy sad tomb not a weed gaily flaunting
　　Could Matilda's devotion permit there should be;
But vile weeds thy path were *once* cruelly haunting,
　　To blight the fair rose that they sicken'd to see.

Yet the thorns of contempt, with mild dignity arming,
　　Kept aloof the base upstarts that sought to molest:
Contempt is to cowards the power disarming,
　　Turns each shaft to a feather, each sting to a *jest*.

Then grant, O great God ! since to Mary 'twas given
  Most perfect among erring mortals to be,
That chief of thy slaves she may serve thee in heaven,
  And bear, when I die, my frail spirit to thee.

THE FEMALE PHILOSOPHER.

YOU tell me, fair one, that you ne'er can love,
   And seem with scorn to mock the dangerous fire;
But why, then, trait'ress, do you seek to move
   In others what *your* breast can ne'er inspire?

You tell me, you my *friend* alone will be,
   Yet speak of friendship in a voice so sweet,
That, while I struggle to be coldly free,
   I feel my heart with wildest throbbings beat.

Vainly indiff'rence would you bid us feel,
   While so much languor in those eyes appear;
Vainly the stoic's happiness reveal,
   While soft emotion all your features wear.

O, form'd for love! O, wherefore should you fly
  From the seducing charm it spreads around?
O why enshrine your soul with apathy?
  Or wish in frozen fetters to be bound?

Life is a darksome and a dreary day,
  The solitary wretch no pleasure knows;
Love is the star that lights him on his way,
  And guides him on to pleasure and repose.

But oft, forgetful of thy plan severe,
  I've seen thee fondly gaze—I've heard thee sigh;
I've mark'd thy strain of converse, sadly dear,
  While softest rapture lighten'd from thine eye.

Then have I thought some wayward youth employ'd
  Thy secret soul, but left thee to despair,
And oft with pleasing sorrow have enjoy'd
  The task of chasing thy corrosive care.

Yet pride must save me from a dastard love,
  A grov'ling love, that cannot hope return:
A soul like mine was never form'd to prove
  Those viler passions with which some can burn.

Then fear not me ; for since it is thy will,

Adhere with stubborn coolness to thy vow ;

Grant me thy philosophic friendship still—

I'll grant thee *mine* with all the powers I know.

END OF THE FIRST VOLUME.

PRINTED BY D. N. SHURY, BERWICK-STREET, SOHO.

HOURS OF SOLITUDE.

VOL. II.

HOURS OF SOLITUDE.

A COLLECTION OF

Original Poems,

NOW FIRST PUBLISHED.

By CHARLOTTE DACRE,
BETTER KNOWN BY THE NAME OF
ROSA MATILDA.

IN TWO VOLUMES.

VOL. II.

Ah! what is mirth but turbulence unholy,
When to the charm compared of heavenly melancholy?

MILTON.

London:
Printed by D. N. SHURY, Berwick-Street, Soho;

FOR HUGHES, WIGMORE-STREET, CAVENDISH-SQUARE;
AND RIDGEWAY, PICCADILLY.

1805.

HOURS OF SOLITUDE.

THE MOTHER

To her Sleeping Infant.

SEE the beauteous baby smiling
   In that calm and gentle sleep,
Of its grief my heart beguiling,
   Bidding me forbear to weep.

But, alas! I still must sorrow,
   While I think I still must sigh;
A cruel blight may, ere the morrow,
   Bid my lovely rose-bud die.

Yet should the blight, in pity sparing,
  Pass o'er innocence like thine,
Still I view thee, sad, despairing,
  Lest thy lot resemble mine.

Love may mark thee for delusion,
  Friendship thy young heart deceive,
The world will mock thy soul's effusion,
  Mock the *fool* that could believe.

Ah! sweet babe, in that calm slumber
  Vainly would my soul divine
What varied ills thy days may number,
  What miseries Fate may thee design.

Enthusiast! thou may'st vainly languish,
  O'er the scenes of life refine;
Then art thou doom'd to ceaseless anguish,
  Or distraction must be thine.

Ingratitude will sure pursue thee,
  Persecution be thy doom;
I weep, and while I sadly view thee,
  Think how peaceful is the tomb.

Sleep then, sweet babe, I shall not sorrow;
   Sleep thy halcyon life away;
I need not fear the blight to-morrow,
   'Twill come the sharper for its stay.

ALAS! FORGIVE ME.

You say you once lov'd me, and lov'd me to madness,
    But ah! are you sure that you felt as you said?
Or could you, unmov'd, see me thus plung'd in sadness;
    Unmov'd, could you see all my feelings betray'd?

To punish me thus for a moment of folly,
    Is far from a gentle, a sensitive mind;
And surely such ages of deep melancholy
    May blot out a *moment* when reason was blind.

Think, think of my sorrow, my unfeign'd emotion,
    When coldly you said that you lov'd me no longer;
Discard then, I pray you, discard the false notion,
    Which tells you that *weak* is the love which is *stronger*.

If e'er you believ'd I was blest with perception,
  To distinguish a spark from the light of the sun,
O ! how could you ever admit the conception,
  Another could charm me where *you* had made one.

Then doom me no longer to deep preying anguish,
  And doom me no longer your loss to bewail;
For your *talents,* your *genius,* your *converse* I languish,
  Ah ! let o'er your coldness my wishes prevail.

Those eyes which so lately you gaz'd on with pleasure,
  Ah ! how can you see them o'erflowing with tears ?
I feel that a *sensitive* being's a treasure,
  Who pays in possession the wishes of years,

Then oh ! well consider, before your rejection,
  Philosophy ne'er can diminish a loss,
The value of which is discern'd on reflection,
  Unalloy'd, except by an *atom* of dross.

Yet if with cold caution, my softness despising,
  You turn from me *still* with fastidious reserve,
Believe tho' now slumb'ring, my pride swift arising,
  Its dignity then shall know how to preserve.

I well know that pride would disdain my confession,

But *I* love not the pride which forbids me to feel ;

More noble the glory to lighten oppression,

And wound one's own bosom, *another*'s to heal.

THE REPLY.

When I swore that I lov'd you, and lov'd you to
  madness,
  My words they were broken, my eyes overflow'd ;
When you own'd that *you* lov'd, my heart bounded
  with gladness,
  I felt of my bliss as the bliss of a god.

Again what I felt, when in languishing posture
  You heard from *another* the tale that *he* loved,
'Twas a pang so sublim'd, of such exquisite torture,
  As tyrants inflict not, nor victims have prov'd.

You say, with a sigh and a tear, it was folly,
  Enough, my sweet * * * *, no more I despair,
That sigh of confession has chas'd melancholy,
  That tear of contrition has wash'd away care.

On those eyes let me gaze, on that breast let me languish,
　　Till utterance is faint, and the fire of the eye
Can alone speak the passion that rises to anguish,
　　That throbs at the heart, and exhales in a sigh.

Be blest then to-day, come what may come to-morrow,
　　Exchang'd be our sighs, let our tears overflow;
For sighs are not always the children of sorrow,
　　And tears are the tribute to rapture we owe.

AZOR.*

* For the poems signed AZOR I am indebted to a gentleman.

To ————

My Reason for being one Week absent from her.

You ask me why my throbbing breast
    Heaves with a rising sigh ;
You ask me why the glist'ning tear
    Stands trembling in my eye :

Forbear, fond love, the *cause* to seek,
    That fills these tearful eyes ;
Forbear the reason to inquire,
    That bids these sorrows rise.

Of thee possest, whose noble breast
    Each finer feeling warms ;
Of thee possest, whose angel form
    My ravish'd senses charms ;

No fears immediate shake my breast ;
    But thoughts of *future fate*
Instil the salutary dread
    Of happiness too great.

This then alone the secret cause
    That wakes the rising woe ;
This, this alone the secret grief
    That makes my eyes o'erflow.

'Tis the religious awe of love
    Which prompts the sudden flight ;
The *pang* endur'd, the off'ring made,
    Again you bless my sight.

The Samian* thus who felt his bliss
    Above a mortal's rise,
Threw from his hand the gem he priz'd,
    To Fate a sacrifice.

AZOR.

---

* The King of Samos, the events of whose life had been most fortunate, threw into the sea the ring which he most valued, as a sacrifice to fortune ; shortly after the ring was found in a fish which was intended for his table.

TO HER I LOVE.

Oh! no, not lovelier looks the muse,
  In fiction's gaudy colours drest;
'Tis but the heartless bard's excuse,
  'Twas but the apostate* poet's zest.

Who like yon sightless seer† can raise
  Of raptur'd song the strain sublime?
Who sing like him th' immortal's praise,
  While truth and Heav'n attest the rhime?

I own, thy wildest paths among
  Together, Fancy, have we stray'd;
Together fram'd the simple song,
  Inscrib'd to some fictitious maid.

* Waller.   † Milton.

But now when she to whom I bend,
　To whom I raise th' adoring eye,
For whom my earliest pray'rs ascend,
　For whom shall heave my latest sigh ;

O! now when she whose purple bloom
　Transcends the hue th' heav'ns dissolve,
What time the sun dispels the gloom,
　And gems with dew th' op'ning rose ;

O! now when she whose eyes more bright
　Than shine those dew drops to the day,
Direct on me their beaming light,
　And mock the diamond's fainter ray ;

O! now when she whose purest blood
　Speaks in her cheeks, whose form so wrought,
As if with wond'rous soul endued,
　And gifted with the pow'r of thought ;

O! now when pouring on the ear
　That strain of force the soul to thrill,
To tempt an angel from his sphere,
　And bid the vagrant air be still ;

O ! now when *she* descends from Heav'n,
　At once my rapture and my theme,—
Say could I hope to be forgiven,
　And sing of some poetic dream?

Let those whose sickly fancies chase
　In fictious song the phantom fair ;
Ixion like their cloud embrace,
　And find no lovely substance there.

I sing of plighted love and truth,
　Of rapturous hope and fond desire;
Such themes my glowing numbers suit,
　To such I string my living lyre.

That lyre, and all its sounds be thine,
　Oft as its silver chords among
My hand shall stray, and soul incline
　To raise the melody of song.

For, ****, 'tis to thee I owe,
　That love and beauty crown my day ;
Thine therefore be the strains that flow,
　And thine the tributary lay.

SONG.

The Metamorphosis.

Of late I saw thee gay,
  Thine eyes with lustre shone,
Oh! gentle shepherd, say,
  Thy mirth, where is it flown?

Of late I saw thee laughing,
  Thy jovial friends among,
The brilliant goblet quaffing,
  The wildest of the throng.

But now, alas! 'tis passing strange,
  Thy mirth is fled away;
The reason of the mystic change,
  Oh! prythee, prythee say.

Perhaps that I thine ills may cure,

Yet should my aid prove vain,

I'll teach thee *patience to endure,*

Of hopeless love the pain !

IN ANSWER.

Says * * * * O! where is that brilliancy flown,
    Which forbad the intrusion of care ?
That spark evanescent so lately that shone,
    Now yields to the gloom of despair.

Her eyes they *laugh malice* while slily she speaks,
    And affects to inquire what she knows ;
Her heart well can answer the question she seeks,
    And the cause whence that sorrow arose.

Let the flash of fierce triumph illumine that eye,
    That can spurn at the dying or dead,
But far be from * * * * the barbarous joy
    To exult o'er the wretch she has made.

To boist'rous humour I ne'er make pretence,
    For vivacity merely is mine;
And this I employ'd, tho' poor the defence,
    'Gainst the magic of glances like thine.

You saw 'twas not humour, nor wit, nor yet whim,
    And bade the false lustre expire;
Expos'd to such glances, like paste it grew dim,
    And lost all its polish by fire.

Ah! turn then, sweet tempter, those glances away,
    Which, blazing most fiercely, consume;
I'll *try*, since you bid me, I'll try to be gay,
    And the ease which I feel not assume.

I will hum you the tune, and repeat you the lay,
    And tell you the tale you like best;
And thus like the nightingale perch'd on the spray,
    I will sing with a *thorn* at my breast.

                              AZOR.

THE CONFESSION.

ALAS! I fear I cannot longer steel
   My heart against the magic of thy pow'r;
Unusual flutt'rings in my breast I feel,
   And new emotions struggling ev'ry hour.

O! thou, most delicate, and most refin'd,
   'Tis sacrilege to say I *fear* to love
A being, gifted thus with charms of mind,
   So form'd that passion to inspire and prove.

But, traitor! wherefore teach my heart to burn,
   Round which the stream of apathy did flow?
Ah! wherefore bid the freezing current turn,
   And leave that heart with Etna's fires to glow?

Say, was it by the light'ning of thine eyes,
  Which, mine encount'ring, so my soul inflam'd?
Or did thy glowing breath, with magic sighs,
  Enkindle mischief more than may be nam'd?

Mischief indeed!—but ah! I would not change
  Mischief so sweet for all the world could give;
So vile a slave I'm grown, I would not range
  Beyond my chain, nor liberty receive.

Thou gazest on me, and thy gaze but serves
  Thro' all my veins to send tumultuous sweets;
And at thy touch with transports thrill my nerves,
  My bosom with increas'd emotion beats.

Yes, yes, I own what 'tis in vain to hide,
  I love thee more than language can express;
Thou'st conquer'd apathy and giant pride;
  And abject wretches, they the conqu'ror bless.

LE VRAI SEUL EST AIMABLE.

HOW soft are the day dreams, how sweet are the
    slumbers
  Of him who reclines on the lap of the muse,
The pow'rs of persuasion await on his numbers,
  And thrill thro' the heart of the woman he woos.

To his eye lie disclos'd all the sweets of creation,
  To him all the beauties of nature are known;
From the lily's pale hue to the gaudy carnation,
  He marks all their tints, and he makes them his own.

Then mingling their colours at fancy's direction,
  A form all angelic his pencil designs;
In the morn's orient crimson he dips for complexion;
  For lustre he dives in the depth of the mines.

From thee, lovely rose, as thy charms are disclosing,
   He snatches the buds that just ope to the view,
On her bosom ingrafts them, where sweetly reposing,
   The eye is delighted by contrast of hue.

Erect as a cedar, yet such in proportion
   As painters have pencil'd the mother of Love;
The stag when he bounds not so graceful in motion,
   In sweetness of aspect all painting above.

Such she for whose picture he rifles all nature,
   Transferring each charm to the form he pourtrays;
Thus perfect in figure, in air, and in feature,
   He calls on mankind for their tribute of praise.

To phantoms unreal he claims no devotion,
   For true is the portrait, and lovely the fair,
As ever inspir'd the fond heart with emotion,
   Or wip'd from the forehead the damp of despair.

Forgive then, sweet * * * *, the innocent fiction,
   That drew as from fancy the charms that are thine;
For sketching those charms I but sooth the affliction
   Which harrows in absence this bosom of mine.

c 3   Azor

ˋA L'OREILLER DE MA MAITRESSE.

SWEET pillow! on whose down the loveliest fair
   That e'er in slumber clos'd her radiant eyes,
Reclines, her wasted spirits to repair,
   That, hence recruited, lovelier she may rise:
Oh! say, as morn dissolves the airy dream,
What lover is the fair one's waking theme?

Yes, sweetest pillow, from the wings of Love
   Was dropt thy down, that woos her to repose,
Or else the plumage of his mother's dove
   Was lent, thy envied softness to compose:
Accept, sweet pillow, a fond lover's kiss,
E'en while I breathe a sigh to share thy bliss.

What beauties from my ardent gaze conceal'd,

   What graces to thee carelessly expos'd,

What charms to thee, and *thee alone* reveal'd,

   Disrobing   * * * *   matchless form disclos'd :

What time the sun had sunk beneath the main,

To her the hour of rest, to me of pain.

Ah! paint that form of perfect symmetry,

   In nature's mould of elegance design'd,

The blush that mantles, and the sparkling eye,

   Whose piercing radiance speaks th' enlighten'd mind.

Ah! paint that bosom swelling to the sight,

Where the eye wanders with disturb'd delight.

Yet hold;   can *words* those glowing charms express?

   The Muse indignant leaves th' imperfect strain;

Painting its feeble efforts must confess,

   E'en fancy strives to sketch, but strives in vain :

Ah! pillow, lovelier is the weight you bear;

Than painter's tint, than poet's dream, more fair.

Say then, to thee her secret thoughts are known,

   When night descends, ere sleep assails her eyes,

What lover's name escapes in falt'ring tone?

   Why heaves her breast? why do her blushes rise?

Oh! deign th' envied secret to resign;

Say that she names, and that the name is *mine.*

So may'st thou still her faultless form survey,

   When sleep her beamy orbs shall set in night,

Soon to awake, to emulate the day,

   And fill the world with wonder and delight;

So may her bosom on thy down recline,

Nor be its weight remov'd, but when it leans on mine.

                        AZOR.

THE DOUBT.

HOW wild is the struggle, how deep is the anguish
   That preys on my bosom, by fancy refin'd ;
I feel in this torture I long cannot languish,
   A torture that springs from a *doubt* in the mind.

I feel, and I feel it with deep melancholy,
   Impure is the passion I cherish for thee ;
My lover, oh! speak, is my flame not unholy ?
   O! speak, and thy voice shall be *conscience* to me.

O! speak thou, and calm me, thy words like the show'r
   Arabia's scorch'd desarts descending to cheer,
Shall soon, by their soft, their enliv'ning pow'r,
   Refresh th' hot soul that exhales not a tear.

O! this *right* and this *wrong*, it can ne'er be ideal,
    Nor fancy, nor priestcraft, as sceptics would say;
Yet whatever the case, sure the tortures are real,
    Which harass the wretch who finds *doubt* on the way.

O! how my heart beats, how I start, how I tremble,
    If lonely I wake in the stillness of night,
I see round my bed shadowy visions assemble,
    Their air is forlorn, and their garments not bright.

Ah! these are the spirits of *doubt* that surround me,
    Their voices, now moaning, now whisp'ring, I hear;
Their looks are unsettl'd, their gestures confound me,
    Their figures that change in the mist are not clear.

Such, such is my soul, oh! my friend, oh! my brother,
    Too great between virtue, and love is the strife,
Then I'll yield my best hopes at the feet of another,
    And if I *must* love, it shall prey on my life.

HOW CANST THOU DOUBT?

ALAS! for that voice which the * envoy of Heaven,
  In accents celestial, pour'd sweet on the ear,
That when the song ceas'd, to its spell it was giv'n,
  Attention to fix, as still seeming to hear.

Oh! might such persuasion belong to my numbers,
  As dwelt on the lips of the angel of light,
No more should these phantoms intrude on thy slum-
      bers,
  Or vex with their terrors the dream of the night.

* Raphael. Milton, Book the Eighth.

When the mind is distracted, oft visions obtrusive
   Collect round the couch, and appear to the eye,
When the frame is disorder'd, oft fancies illusive
   Impose, that the vigor of health would defy.

Shall the fumes of such fancies bewilder our reason,
   Must the pulse cease to throb, or the bosom to glow?
And shall *we* concur in the blasphemous treason
   That Heav'n presents but the chalice of woe?

Can that love be impure which aspires to perfection,
   From all that is vulgar and sordid refin'd?
Can that flame be unholy which lights an affection,
   Expanding the heart and enlarging the mind?

Too well sure we feel, could our *wills* have decided,
   Our lives, like our souls, had been blended in one,
But Fate too untoward, our lot has divided,
   Let Fate then account for the work it has done.

But whence is that ray which thro' the gloom brightens,
   And scatters its radiance the meadows among?
'Tis the torch of the glow-worm that nightly enlightens,
   And shines for the elves as they trip it along.

Oh ! no, that fond light which in splendid profusion,
 Effulgent she flings the soft foliage between,
She wastes not, to aid superstitious illusion,
 It shews her wing'd mate where she glows in the
  green*.

Yes this is the law, the fond law of each nature,
 Attracting, attracted to fly to its kind ;
Yes, this is the secret, kind instinct of nature,
 To choose what is best for its pleasure design'd.

Accurst was that prince†, who in horrible union,
 Ordain'd that the living and dead should be join'd ;
But man has decreed the more hateful communion
 Which fetters two souls of dissimilar kind.

Oh! man, foolish man, shall thy skill be exerted
 The laws which creation obeys to controul ?
Shall the order of nature by thee be inverted ?
 And would'st thou enchain what is freest,—the soul ?

 * It is ascertained by naturalists that the light emitted by the light of the glow-worm serves to indicate to its mate on the wing where this brilliant insect reposes.

 † Mezentius, according to Virgil, ordered the living and the dead to be joined together.

Know its spirit, disdaining restriction, sententious,
   Its right shall assert to select and adore,
Unlike in all else to that passion licentious,
   Which seeks what is sensual, and seeks for no more.

O! 'tis only we love, when with souls sweetly blending
   *The thought meets the thought from the lips ere it
       part;
O! 'tis only we love, when with passion transcending
   The hope and the wish spring alike from the heart.

Then thus let us live, and in death lie together,
   Embracing, embrac'd, let the light'ning consume;
Our spirits shall range thro' the fields of pure ether,
   Our ashes together repose in the tomb.

                   AZOR.

* Pope's Eloisa.

THE MISTRESS

To the Spirit of her Lover,

Which, in the phrenzy occasioned by his loss, she imagined to pursue continually her footsteps.

Attempted after the manner of Ossian.

The spirit of my lover pursues me in the wild; I fancy to see his wan figure at my side; he follows me, and speaks in a low murmuring voice. His form is habited in robes of mist, and his silvery hair undulates upon the gale.

Oh! my love, let me hear thy voice when I seek repose; let me not, when I close my eyes, lose sight of thy heavenly form. Be present still to my fond view, and let me never miss thee from my side.

Ah! thou dost not breathe; yet sometimes methinks upon my glowing cheek I feel thy breath, but it is cold and damp, not ardent as in the days of our love.

Can I not press thee to my bosom? Oh! miserable mockery! thou would'st evaporate in my embrace.

Yet do not quit me. Thy features are sunk and wan; they diminish to my troubled sight; yet they are a faint resemblance unto the charms of my beloved; and thy hair, which seems luminous, falls over thy shadowy form.

Sometimes thy features seem to waver—it must be in the twilight, when all has a dubious shade; but I cannot always catch those loved features—it appears to me as though they were fading wholly away; but suddenly, by an effort of the imagination, I again identify them, and secretly determine never more to look off of them.

How celestial dost thou appear, skimming over the tops of the hills. A faint moonbeam catches thy robes of silvery mist. I respire eagerly the bleak breeze that passes over thy dubious form ; I inhale it with ardent, melancholy delight, for it is impregnated with thy spirit.

Soon will this heart of clay cease to beat ; then will *my* soul too be free. My body, which is of concentrated atoms, shall lie by thine in the narrow grave, which it will not deny me to share with it; and then together shall our spirits wander over the mountains, or re-visit the scenes of our youth.

THE MISTRESS

To the Spirit of her Lover.

VERSIFIED.

Wilt thou follow me into the wild?
　　Wilt thou follow me over the plain?
Art thou from earth or from heaven exil'd?
　　Or how comes thy spirit at large to remain?

Vision of beauty, vision of love,
　　Follow me, follow me over the earth;
Ne'er leave me, bright shadow, wherever I rove,
　　For dead is my soul to the accents of mirth.

Thou formest my pleasure, thou formest my pain;
　　I see thee, but wo is my eye-sight to me;
Thy heavenly *phantom* doth near me remain,
　　But ah! thy *reality* where shall I see?

In the darkness of night, as I sit on the rock,
  I see a thin form on the precipice brink ;
Oh! Lover illusive, my senses to mock—
  'Tis madness presents if I venture to think.

Unreal that form which now hovers around,
  Unreal those garments which float on the wind,
Unreal those footsteps that touch not the ground,
  Unreal those features, wan vision, I find.

Oh! vain combination !—oh ! embodied mist !
  I dare not to lean on thy transparent form ;
I dare not to clasp thee, tho' sadly I list—
  Thou would'st vanish, wild spirit, and leave me forlorn.

Ah! wilt thou not *fall* from that edge of the steep ?
  The pale moon obliquely shines over the lake ;
The shades are deceptive, below is the deep,
  And I see thy fair form in its clear waters shake.

Yet ah! I forget, *thou* art light as a breath ;
  That aerial form, which no atoms combine,
Might dizzily sport down the abyss of death,
  Or tremble secure on the hazardous line.

That hand unsubstantial, oh! might it but press

    These temples, which beat with the madness of love;

Oh! let, if thou seest my frantic distress,

    Some sign of emotion thy *consciousness* prove.

Lo! see thy dim arms are extending for me;

    Thy soul then exists, comprehends, and is mine;

The life now is ebbing which mine shall set free;

    Ah! I feel it beginning to mingle with thine.

FOG.

MISTY his face, and rueful to behold;
   His eyes like dimly shining stars were seen:
And cloudy vestments did his form enfold,
   Like blue smoke curling in the moonlight sheen.

An hazy circlet on his head he wore,
   Like that which sometimes does the moon surround;
A vapory wand within his hand he bore,
   And conjur'd thick'ning shadows from the ground.

His the delight in early winter morn,
   In yellow robes the loaded air to sway;
'Till, King of day, tho' of his glories shorn,
   The broad, red sun compels him far away.

Seldom from murky fen or lake he'll creep
   In summer, save when dusky eve is nigh;
And then he gains the mountain's shadowy steep,
   Or blends, in distance, ocean with the sky.

WILL-O'-WISP.

This elfin sprite, as ancient legends say,
  Was fairy-born ; on him they did bestow
The art to lead poor villagers astray,
  For an offence some thousand years ago.

This elfin sprite with meteor lantern hies
  Close to the edge of slimy pool or lake ;
Still like an anxious guide before them flies,
  Nor, till some mischief done, does them forsake.

This elfin sprite have many tried to seize,
  Yet in the rash attempt have suffer'd sore ;
With mockery of himself he will them teize,
  Which grasping hard, they see him still before.

Then on to fairy land, in gay despight,
   Upon a zephyr will this elfin ride;
And all the fays do at his lantern light
   Their little torches, and the feast provide.

Now seated round the tulip's ample bowl,
   To jocund elves he doth his wiles betray;
In mirthful glee the hours unheeded roll,
   Till dawn just peeps, then swift they hie away.

MILDEW.

BEHOLD, within that cavern drear and dank,
   Whose walls in rainbow tints so dimly shine,
A wretch, with swollen eyes and tresses lank,
   Does on a heap of mould'ring leaves recline.

Unwholsome dews for ever him surround,
   From his damp couch he scarcely ever hies,
Save when blue vapours, issuing from the ground,
   Lure him abroad, to catch them as they rise.

Or else at eve the dripping rock he loves,
   Or the moist edge of new-dug grave, full well;
To get the sea spray too at night he roves,
   And, gem'd with trickling drops, then seeks his cell.

Such his delights, his green and purple cheek,

    His bloated form, his chill, discolour'd hand

He would not change; and if he guests would seek,

    He steals among the church-yard's grisly band.

WIND.

HATING the gentle zephyrs am'rous sighs,
  Hating the smoothness of the glassy main,
From prison'd cave, impatient to arise,
  He struggles wild, vast freedom to attain.

And when unfetter'd from superiour force,
  He rushes loud the waken'd waters o'er;
Or taking o'er the hills his viewless course,
  Wild echo thro' the woods repeats the roar.

Or when autumnal leaves he scatters far,
  Or mournful sighs the crannied rocks among,
Till dark-rob'd winter mounts her ebon car,
  Then hails his queen, and howls her path along.

For he disdains fair summer's gentle form,

And hates unruffl'd eve in vestments gay ;
He loves to battle in the pelting storm,

And scatter devastation on his way.

FROST.

HIS ruby cheek made orient crimson pale,
His gelid hair did stiffen in the gale;
Like silv'ry wire it glitter'd in the ray,
And scintillating sparklets strew'd his way.

The robe around his frozen body flung
Was dazzling snow, in folds fantastic hung;
A crown of icicles bedeck'd his brow;
His form throughout transparently did show.

Fatal to him the genial breath of spring,
And warning sad her green-rob'd heralds bring;
At night awhile he still maintains his sway,
But soon flies trembling from her footsteps gay.

Toward the high mountain of perpetual snows
He journies on, to take his keen repose,
Where, closely ribb'd in icy fetters bright,
He rests secure upon the slippery height.

THAW.

'TIS she, the nymph with dripping hair,
  Who, when Aquarius rules the sky,
With dewy robes and bosom bare,
  On southern gales delights to hie.

Then with her genial breath create
  New life within the teeming land;
And rescue nature, bound so late
  By winter's adamantine hand.

Thus well her presence gay we deem;
  Before the nymph enchantment flies;
And waken'd beauties conscious seem
  From numbing lethargy to rise.

Awhile she stays ;   when, tripping on,

   Fair spring the sov'reign sway obtains ;

And then she hastes those climes among,

   Where later winter lingering reigns.

THE GIANT'S BURIAL GROUND.

O'ER an immeasurable space, the eye
Saw conic mountains tap'ring to the sky,
And caverns dark as Acheron between,
Vast pits for graves that newly op'd had been,
While on their edge the moon's pale light reveal'd
Huge sculls, but late within the earth conceal'd ;
And giant spectres stalking o'er the glade,
Like moving pyramids of Egypt, stray'd.

The Genii guard, in rueful state reclin'd :
His far-felt sighs seem'd hollow gusts of wind,
His viewless length, on an high heap of bones,
Extended lay ; his deep and echoing moans

Seem'd distant thunder o'er the awe-struck land,

Or bade the mariner fear storms at hand.

IIis tears bright globes, commingling as they fell

Into a river, at his feet did swell,

Which streaming thro' the waste with low'ring roar,

A chorus strange maintains there evermore.

ADDRESSED TO THE AUTHOR

IN THE MORNING HERALD,

By an unknown Hand.

IN ANSWER TO HER LINES INTITLED 'THE PHILOSOPHER.'

'TIS not indiff'rent, I would have you prove;
 Ah! if you love, cherish the sacred fire,
For I'm no traitor, nor would seek to move
 In others, what my breast could not inspire.

If all my features soft emotion wear,
 They truly speak—I feel them in my soul;
Must I love less—if aught—tho' not a fear
 Fetters those feelings, dictates a controul?

The name of friendship I confess is sweet,
  With that you grant me I would never part;
Friendship is thine—with rapture I would meet
  The warmest, wildest throbbings of thy heart.

Friendship is sweet; but love, oh! sweeter still!
  The union gives a source of real joy;
Grant then thy love, and know it is my will
  To give thee happiness without alloy.

WEYMOUTH.

On being prevented by severe illness from going thither.

SWEET spot! it cannot e'er offend I deem,
   That I my solitude to guile
Should chuse thee for the subject of my theme,
   Cheating my fancy with the sketch awhile.

What, tho' forbidden on thy mazy beach
   In silent pensiveness to stray,
Fancy can soar above oppression's reach,
   And in an instant wing the distant way.

But fancy cannot give with equal ease
   All sober certainty might have,
The scent salubrious, nor the balmy breeze,
   Fresh from the saline bosom of the wave.

Yet tell me, gentle spot, why crouds resort
　　To revel oft thy scenes among?
More suited thou for love, or reason's court,
　　Than the gay madness of the giddy throng.

IL TRIONFO DEL AMOR.

SO full my thoughts are of thee, that I swear
   All else is hateful to my troubl'd soul ;
   How thou hast o'er me gain'd such vast controul,
   How *charm'd* my stubborn spirit is most rare.
Sure thou hast mingl'd philtres in my bowl !
   Or what thine high enchanted arts declare
   Fearless of blame—for truth I will not care,
   So charms the witchery, whether fair or foul.
Yet well my love-sick mind thine *arts* can tell ;
   No magic potions gav'st thou, save what I
   Drank from those lustrous eyes when they did dwell
   With dying fondness on me—or thy sigh
Which sent its perfum'd poison to my brain.
   Thus known thy spells, thou bland seducer, see—
   Come practice them again, and oh! again ;
Spell-bound *I am*—and spell-bound *wish* to be.

QUEEN MAB AND HER FAYS,

Transforming themselves into Flies.

LITTLE queen of elves and fays,
Fancy's wand thy charm betrays,
To her musing eye reveal'd,
Tho' in form of fly conceal'd.

The little fairies in thy train
Punctually their parts sustain,
Now they linger in the rear,
A secret scarcely breath'd to hear.

Buzzing nigh the mourning lover,
Soon his hidden grief discover;
Then by dreams inform the fair
Of his long conceal'd despair.

From the love-sick maiden's lip,
Accents scarcely form'd they sip;
From her melting tell-tale eyes
Snatch the wishes as they rise.

Skimming now the studied hays
In the sun's declining rays,
Joining now in wavy ring
On the zephyr's balmy wing.

Little faith would mortals give,
Art in form of fly could live,
Or their figur'd mazy dance
Boast consistence but by chance.

Laden now with precious fare,
To their queen they swift repair;
And, from vapours of the earth,
Bid their slaves, the dreams, come forth.

Now the lover clasps his maid,
Wishes by a vision paid;
Now the maiden yields her charms
To the lover's anxious arms:

Now the grave gives up its prey,
Friends arise, but swift away ;
Dreams disperse, delusions fly,
And shew of sleep the mockery.

Thus, thou little wily queen,
Mortal secrets dost thou glean,
To serve thee for thy gay disport,
In thy small and viewless court.

THE EVIL BEING.

OH! Thou whose breath empoisons the sweet air,
Whose heart is evil, and whose mind despair ;
Whose baleful tongue the fairest fame can blight,
Whose deeds of horror shun the eye of light.

How cam'st thou, fiend, upon this earth to dwell ?
Did thy perturbed spirit rise from hell ?
Or from the close-ribb'd rock in tempest torn?
For thou of woman-kind wert never born !

Look in his aspect—shame ne'er made it glow ;
Enthron'd sits crimson murder on his brow ;
While ambush'd in his fierce demoniac eye,
Fraud, and the baser passions, scowling li !

GRIMALKIN'S GHOST;

OR,

THE WATER SPIRITS.

In humble imitation of the soaring flights of some legendary and exquisitely pathetic modern Bards.

JONAS lay on his bed, so my tale does relate,
And queer were the visions that roam'd in his pate,
 When the clock on the staircase told one;
The door it flew wide, and a light fill'd the room;
Oh! mercy, what now is my horrible doom?
 Thought Jonas—for speech he had none.

He look'd thro' his fingers; and, strange to declare,
He saw such a sight as his senses did scare—
    A Cat, with five kits in her train!
" Ah! monster!" she cried, 'twixt a scream and a mew,
" You thought you had drown'd us, but woe unto you,
    Our spirits have risen again.

" We shall haunt you by day, we shall haunt you by
        night,
Behind and before, at your left and your right,
    No comfort shall ever you know ;
What harm had we done you? base monster, declare,
Tho' each had nine lives, you not any would spare,
    But doom'd us to perish, *oh! oh!*

" Now vengeance is ours, lo ! we wreak it on you;"
The *five little kittens* cried " Mew! mew! mew!"
    And jump'd on poor Jonas's bed ;
They rear'd on their hind legs, they danc'd on his
        breast,
With their cold, tender paws on his windpipe they
        press'd,
    And play'd at *bo-peep* round his head.

Of a sudden they ceas'd, he just ventur'd to peep,
But better for him had he still seem'd asleep,
    For horrid the sight he beheld;
The angry mamma like a leopard was grown,
Her large sea-green eyes fiercely gleam'd on his own,
    And her tail was enormously swell'd.

" Oh! monster," she scream'd, with a cattish despair,
" I am doom'd after death in your torments to share,
    Or vengeance the fates will deny;
Round the brink of a well, such the sentence decreed,
After five *spectre kittens* you swiftly proceed,
    Whilst I spit at your heels as you fly."

THE HUNTER OF THE ALPS.

SEE where on Alpine heights the hunter keen
 Follows the feather-footed chamois's flight,
Now on the brink of fearful abyss seen,
 Now proudly gazing from the slippery height.

His fell pursuer, man, with anxious eye,
 Follows resolv'd—his pointed spike in hand;
His haggard air seems with the scene to vie,
 Nobly forlorn, and desolately grand.

Unceasing from the earliest streak of dawn,
 O'er sheets of ice and dazzling snow he hies;
Now on the dizzy steep by magic borne,
 Now o'er the precipice like light'ning flies.

And oft, if night her sable plumes should spread
  O'er toil unpaid—no lassitude he knows ;
A fragment of the rock supports his head,
  And deaf'ning torrents lull him to repose.

Too happy if at length his prize he gain,
  The fleet chamois—whose wild, disdainful eye,
Whose graceful form, whose slender feet are vain—
  The hunter's glory is to bid him die !

These are the strange delights of savage life!
  Yet tender ties the mountain warrior knows,
A cottage, children, and a gentle wife!
  For whom, while braving death, his bosom glows.

Yet such a life hath charms—its enterprise,
  Its constant animation, and its care,
Gives birth to energy—bids hope arise,
  And saves the soul from torpor and despair.

SONG OF MELANCHOLY.

DARK as the wintry midnight is my soul; sad and tempestuous. Fain would I sit upon the stern brow'd rock, listening to the roaring of the terrible cataract.

Fool! to endure life, wandering, as I do, in the solitary path, while gloomy shadows stalk in the dim mist, and point at me with melancholy gesture.

I come, I come, gloomy shadows!—I hasten to be disembodied.

Bitter shrieks the North wind over the mountains; the night-bird screams dismal o'er the dark green yew. Oh! let me be laid in the grave, and let the spirits of the air bend over my tomb!

I am unfit for the world; black misery pervades my brain; the desart of gloom suits my soul. The wild blast driving the heavy clouds over the mountains —the dreamy din of midnight chorus, oppressing the soul with deadly and mysterious sorrow, best befits me —the forgotten of Heaven!

Man is the monster from whose jaws I fly! whose poison'd arrow still festers in my heart, and defies the skill of the physician.

Spirit of death! bear me from the scene of my woe! all night will I watch for thee on the cold tomb-stone. Take pity, and receive me among ye—stretch forth from the slowly yawning tomb your slender arms, spirits of the quiet dead!

Oh! what have I done, that dreadful woe should haunt my footsteps? What have I done, that the phantom of despair should fly before me, shrieking and wringing her lurid hands?

Oh! let me die, that my sorrows may rest in the tomb—that the voice of man may strike never more upon my maddened brain, and that the innocent smile of * * * * * may never mock the bursting of my sad heart.

God of Heaven! I beseech thee for death; stop, in pity, stop the feverish beating of my heart—let not my own hand urge the life away. Yet never can the tempest of my mind be quell'd—the stormy ocean may be easier to appease! I feel in my soul that happiness can never more return. Sad and strange are my nights; my days are a dim mist. Smile on me, oh! God! and send thy pale angel, Death, to bear me away in his arms.

Bitter shrieks the North wind over the mountains; the night-bird screams dismal from the dark green yew. Oh! let me be laid in the grave, and let the spirits of the air bend over my tomb!

L' ABSENCE.

HAST thou not seen the blooming rose
　Turn to the God of day?
Her fragrant treasures all disclose,
　Enchanted by his ray?

Hast thou not seen the sun decline!
　Her bloomy beauty fade;
And joyless of his warmth divine,
　Soon perish in the shade?

How say'st thou, love? thy bosom glows,
　Bereft of *thee*, I fade;
My vanish'd sun—thy drooping rose
　Will perish in the shade.

Thou art my sun—thou **art my dew,**
   Spirit by which **I live !**
Come swift then, and a life renew,
   To which thou *soul* cans't give !

THE APPARITION.

AS slow I wander'd o'er yon barren heath,
    Musing on woes to come—on evils past,
    Cursing that fate me in such mould had cast,
I at my side did hear a gentle breath!
When straitway looking down, behold I saw
    A piteous imp—deform'd his limbs appear'd,
    And wither'd quite—while on a stick he rear'd
His wretched weight—on nature's face a flaw!
Pale was his ashy cheek—no hope there beam'd
    From his sunk eye; his matted locks, poor child!
    O'er his mishapen back hung loose and wild,
And conscious of his misery he seem'd.
Loud blew the wind, and shook the slender wight;
    With long, thin hand he grasp'd his stick, and rais'd
    On me his tearful eyes; sadly I gaz'd,
When swift he vanish'd from my troubl'd sight!

TU ES BEAU COMME LE DESERT, AVEC TOUTES SES FLEURS ET TOUTES SES BRISES.

Oh! my soul's lord! to my enamour'd eye
   A fairer person lives not ;——turn not then
In soft confusion from me—nor deny
   Mine eyes to gaze on thee alone of men.

Thy perfect form, of atoms pure combin'd,
   Fair habitation for a lovely soul,
Seeming too much for mortal-clay refin'd,
   Such bright effulgence mantles thro' the whole.

Thy gentle aspect doth thy mind reveal,
   Such love, such harmony, such thoughts benign,
That from me my impassion'd soul does steal,
   As anxious to identify with thine!

Oh! delicate seductions! thine alone—

  By nature granted *thee* all men above,

And ah! I trust to all but me unknown,

  Whose spirit was sent forth with thine to move.

For sure I own I could not calmly bear

  Another should thine essence comprehend,

Nor e'er attempt in *thought* of thee to share,

  Who doth so far above all thought transcend !

Ambrosial air doth ever thee surround

  Thy proper atmosphere—its pow'r I feel

With such strange influence as persuades me well,

  Near me thou com'st, tho' sight may not reveal.

Then ah! believe these sacred sympathies—

  These links divine, we still should dread to sever ;

Remember that when *nature* in us dies,

  Our *souls* unshackl'd spring to life for ever.

LASSO A ME!

ALAS for me!—ah! would that it were true
  I did not love thee—tyrant, then would I
  With calmness bear thy taunting jealousy,
  Thy looks severe—thy cold averted eye,
And bear, without an anguish'd smile, to view
Attentions paid where ne'er they can be due.
  Ah! then would I in pride of heart suppress
  The rising sigh—in joyous garb so dress
  My features all—that none my grief should guess.
This would I do, but that I love too well
  By haughtiness in bitter kind to pay
  Those cruel doubts, that o'er thee have such sway,
  And so our moments vex ;—that sooth to say,
'Twere better die than thus in mis'ry dwell—
Thy burning jealousies our mutual hell!

Alas for me!—if thou wilt not believe
My heart is only thine—then, tyrant, take
 Thy poignard, and at once thy *mind* relieve ;
For thine own image—thou a tomb wilt make,

THE WARRIOR.

Originally addressed to a Young Gentleman, who, entering under the banners of Mars, signalized himself in the service of his country. On his return he was, as is generally the fate of heroes, entangled by the snares of Venus; this led to the commission of numberless indiscretions, which ultimately threw him out of his situation in the army. As nothing, however, could fade the laurels he had acquired, the authoress of these pages addressed to him the subsequent Ode in the year 1802, since which he unfortunately fell a martyr to his too enthusiastic courage and thirst for distinction, in the memorable engagement in Egypt, which proved the awful mausoleum of so many heroes.

> AH! shall th' enamour'd muse recite
> Thy vent'rous glories gain'd in fight?
> When following fierce the din of war,
> Lur'd by Bellona's trump from far,

Thy men victorious onward led
  O'er many a smoking field,
And chang'd to heroes !—freely bled
  Near thee, asham'd to yield.

Or drooping low her soaring wing,
Falt'ring touch a sadder string,
Weeping, shall she not relate
The harsh decrees of stubborn fate ?
Sinking from embattl'd story,
  How, with many a wound aggriev'd,
Weep that form which speaks thy glory,
  Scars alone should have atchiev'd !

Yet viewing thee with grief inspir'd,
Again she feels her fancy fir'd ;
Again with rapture loves to trace
Th' immortal glories of thy race :
She *sees* the hero of her lay,
  While mem'ry points to fame,
All lesser regrets fade away,
  For Triumph marks his name !

When erst a youth, thy dawning years
Fill'd all around with hopes and fears;
Courage and Virtue were combin'd,
But Vanity still intertwin'd:
From Passion all thine errors sprung,
   Luxuriant nature's child!
For Passion o'er thy reason flung
   Her chain of flow'rets wild.

Vainly to stop thy wild career,
Had Prudence caution'd thee to fear,
Like some bright comet darting by
The lesser spangles of the sky,
Thy course no more might be detain'd,
   Tho' boding evil near,
But onward *still* would be maintain'd,
   Destruction in the rear.

Thy fame victorious early swell'd,
America thy feats beheld;
To raise the youthful warrior's pride,
Fortune her various honours tried!

Homage in all thy footsteps trod,

  In ev'ry clime and state,

In crouds to look and move the god—

  Ah! 'twas a test *too* great!

The hero fell;—ah! muse forbear,

Forbear to shed th' ignoble tear:

Phaeton, who sought to rule the world,

For vanity was downward hurl'd.

A mortal is a mortal still,

  Whate'er the prize he gain;

He hath not *pow'r*, but only *will*,

  Perfection to attain.

Then weep not, Muse, thy fav'rite's fall,

Misfortune is the lot of all;

And Merit, struggling with its foes,

But *prouder* from oppression grows;

Then baleful Envy hovers round,

  To blast the soldier's wreath,

To rob the brows with honour crown'd,

  Nor leave him fame in death!

True, hate unkind and slander foul
Combine to crush the soaring soul,
But, like a bright and vig'rous flame,
It *still* shall rise to gild thy name,
Confuse, expose the ranc'rous band,
　　And shine in triumphs new,
Their lowliest rev'rence *yet* command
　　The friendship of a few.

Then hasten, youth! from British clime,
Let blushing honours croud thy time!
Haste! and shortly be repaid
Those glories thou did'st rashly fade;
Retire awhile, let Malice spend
　　Its idle rage and hate,
And Providence shall be thy friend,
　　And mindful of thy fate.

Shadows in youth we all pursue,
Covet the false, disdain the true;
Passion in her trappings vain,
Lures the hero to his bane;

But pale Experience, sternly keen,
  Points out youthful folly,
Then, amaz'd, we quit the scene,
  To mourn in melancholy.

It *cannot* be, a day so bright
Should sink in endless gloomy night;
It cannot be, so bright a morn
Of all its glories should be shorn!
It *must not* be, a noon so glorious
  Clouds eternal should o'ercast,
Nor thy laurel-wreath victorious
  Perish in the envious blast!

Then let, oh! Muse, thy tears be dry,
While Hope forbids the rising sigh—
I tell thee, tho' a cruel blow
Threw thy comely hero low;
His eve in glitt'ring vest shall smile,
  Dispers'd the transient gloom,
And gaily to his native isle
  Bright beams his path illume!

WE CAN LOVE BUT ONCE.

TRUANT! you love me not—the reason this,
  You told me that you lov'd a maid before;
And tho', perchance, you many more may kiss,
  True love, felt *once*, can never be felt *more*.
  Then ask not me to credit what you swore,
Nor e'er believe that I can give you bliss;
  Go, go to her who taught you how to love—
  Repeat to *her* your vows, and not to me;
For sooth I think, who can inconstant prove
  To his *first* love, will ever faithless be.
  In gaining wayward hearts no pride I see,
Nor have I pride in kindling in the breast
  That *meteor* flame, call'd passion—no not I;
The *heart* I aim at, and of that possess'd,
  Make it my castle, and all arts defy,
  For that once fill'd—no longer roves the eye.

IT may be proper to state, that a translation of the Poem which bears the title of " The Lass of Fair Wone," from the German of Bürger, I once met with in a periodical publication four or five years ago; conceiving it extremely interesting, but yet susceptible of some improvement, I ventured to make in it such alterations as I flattered myself, without deducting from the sense or substance of the original, might render it, in some measure, more acceptable to the English reader; for the Germans, in an overstrain'd attempt at nature, often pourtray her in her worst and plainest garb. The heroine in the poem alluded to, after perpetrating the murder of her infant, is made to finish her career at the gallows. To run a pin through the heart of a new-born babe, and be hung for the action, I judged an event, however justly conceived, too familiarly disgustful to require an excuse for its suppression.

Whether or not I have succeeded in the wish of improving, by any attempt of mine, the translation of this poem, *I* must leave to the decision of *those who* are most capable of judging; *at the same time* hoping it will be fully understood *I* am far from claiming any merit on *so trifling an occasion.*

I have subjoined a few stanzas as *specimens of the* translation to which *I have alluded.*

SPECIMEN OF THE FORMER TRANSLATION

OF

THE LASS OF FAIR WONE.

HER sire, a harsh and angry man,
  With furious voice revil'd,
" Hence from my sight, I'll none of thee—
  I harbour not thy child."

And fast amid her fluttering hair,
  With clenched fist he gripes,
And seized a leathern thong, and lash'd
  Her side with sounding stripes.

———

" Poor soul, I'll have thee hous'd and nurs'd ;
  Thy terrors I lament:
Stay here—we'll have some further talk—
  The old one shall repent :

What's fit and fair I'll do for thee,
  Shalt yet retain my love—
Shalt wed my huntsman, and we'll then
  Our former transports prove.

———

" Me vengeance waits ; my poor, poor child,
  Thy wound shall bleed afresh,
When ravens from the gallows tear
  Thy mother's mould'ring flesh."

Hard by the bow'r her gibbet stands ;
  Her skull is still to show ;
It seems to eye the barren grave,
  Three spans in length below.

THE LASS OF FAIR WONE.

From the German of Bürger.

BESIDE the parson's dusky bow'r*
  Why strays a troubl'd sprite,
That dimly shines in lonely hour
  Thro' curtains of the night?

Why steals along yon slimy bank
  An hov'ring fire so blue,
That lights a spot both drear and dank,
  Where falls nor rain nor dew?

---

* In the translation to which I have already alluded, the lines
only rhime alternately; wherever I have added an entire stanza
I have marked the passage by an asterisk.

The parson once a daughter had,
  Fair village maids above ;
Unstain'd as fair—and many a lad
  Had sought the maiden's love.

High o'er the hamlet proudly dight
  Beyond the winding stream,
The windows of yon mansion bright
  Shone in the evening beam.

A Bacchanalian lord dwelt there,
  Unworthy of his name ;
He plung'd a father in despair,
  And robb'd a maiden's fame.

With wine and tapers sparkling round,
  The night flew swift away ;
In huntsman's dress, with horn and hound,
  He met the dawning day.

He sent the maid his picture, deck'd
  With diamonds, pearls, and gold ;
Ah ! silly maid, why not reject
  What on the back was told?

" Despise the love of shepherd boys;
   Shalt thou be basely woo'd
That worthy art of highest joys,
   And youths of noble blood?

" The tale I would to thee unfold
   In secret must be said;
And when the midnight hour is told,
   Fair love, be not afraid.

" And when the am'rous nightingale
   Like thee shall sweetly sing,
A stone thy window shall assail,
   My idol forth to bring."

Attired in vest of gayest blue,
   He came with lonely tread,
And silent as the beams that threw
   Their pale light o'er her head.

And did no thought affect his breast,
   Or bid his feet delay?
Ah! no! the crime but adds a zest
   To spur his guilty way.

And when the sweet-pip'd nightingale
   Sang from the dusky bow'r,
A stone her window did assail
   Just at the midnight hour.

And ah! she came;—his treacherous arms
   The trembling maid receive;
How soon do they in lover's charms
   A lover's truth believe!

* Lock'd in his arms, she scarcely strove,
   Seduc'd by young desire,
The glowing twin brother of Love,
   Possess'd with wilder fire.

Still struggling, faint, he led her on
   Tow'rd the fatal bow'r,
So still—so dim—while all along
   Sweet smelt each blushing flow'r.

Then beat her heart—and heav'd her breast—
   And pleaded ev'ry sense;
Remorseless the seducer prest,
   To blast her innocence.

But soon in tears repentant drown'd,
　The drooping fair bemoan'd,
And oft, when night in terror frown'd,
　Forlorn and sad she roam'd.

And when the fragrile flow'rs decay'd,
　The bloom her cheeks forsook,
And from her eyes no longer play'd
　The loves with wily look.

* And when the leaves of autumn fell,
　And grey the grass was grown,
Her bosom rose with lovely swell,
　And tighter grew her zone.

And when the mow'rs went a field
　The yellow corn to ted,
She felt her sorrowing bosom yield
　To all a mother's dread.

And when the winds of winter swept
　The stubborn glebe among,
In wild despair and fear she wept
　The lingering night along.

And when the fault of yielding love
   No more could be conceal'd,
She knelt, her father's soul to move,
   And, weeping, all reveal'd.

† But vain her tears ; the ruthless sire
   In piteous voice revil'd,
And while his eye-balls flash'd with fire,
   He spurn'd his hapless child :

Spurn'd her with cruelty severe,
   And smote her snowy breast;
The patient blood, that gush'd so clear,
   Its purity confess'd.

* Such are the dang'rous thorns of love,
   That strew the virgin's way,
While faithless as its roses prove,
   'Tis they that first decay.

Then drove her forth forlorn to wail
   Amid the dreary wild,
Forgets that mortals all are frail,
   But more—forgets his child !

† See specimen of former translation.

* Unhappy parent!—passion's slave!
　　Had nature been thy guide,
Thy child, now sunk in hasten'd grave,
　　'Might still have been thy pride.

Up the harsh rock so steep and slim'd,
　　The mourner had to roam,
And faint on tott'ring feet she clim'd
　　To seek her lover's home.

" Alas! my blood-stain'd bosom see,"
　　The drooping sufferer cried;
" A *mother* hast thou made of me,
　　Before thou mad'st a *bride.*

" This is thy ruthless deed—behold!"
　　And sinking on the floor;
" Oh! let thy love with honour hold,
　　My injur'd name restore."

† " Poor maid! I grieve to see thy woe;
　　My folly now lament:
Go not while harsh the tempests blow,
　　Thy father shall repent."

　　† See specimen of former translation.

"I cannot stay," she shudd'ring cried,
  " While dubious hangs my fame.
Alas! forswear thy cruel pride,
  And leave me not to shame.

"Make me thy wife, I'll love thee true;
  High Heaven approves the deed;
For mercy's sake some pity shew,
  E'en while for thee I bleed!"

"Sure 'tis thy mirth, or dost thou rave?
  "Can I," he scoffing cried,
"Thy forfeit name from scorn to save,
  E'er wed a peasant maid?

"What honour bids I'll do for thee—
  My huntsman shall be thine;
While still our loves, voluptuous free,
  No shackles shall confine."

"Damn'd be thy soul, and sad thy life,
  May pangs in hell await!
Wretch! if too humble for thy wife,
  Oh, why not for thy mate?

" May God attend my bitter prayer !
    Some high-born spouse be thine,
Whose wanton arts shall mock thy care,
    And spurious be thy line.

" Then traitor fell, how wretched those
    In hopeless shame immers'd,
Strike thy hard breast with vengeful blows,
    While curses from it burst !

" Roll thy dry eyes, for mercy call,
    Unsooth'd thy grinning woe ;
Through thy pale temples fire the ball,
    And sink to fiends below !"

Then starting up, she wildly flew,
    Nor heard the hissing sleet,
Nor knew how keen the tempest blew,
    Nor felt her bleeding feet.

" Oh where, my God ! where shall I roam ?
    For shelter where shall fly ?"
She cried, as wild she sought the home
    Where still she wish'd to die.

Tow'rd the bow'r, in frenzied woe,
 The fainting wand'rer drew,
Where wither'd leaves and driving snow
 Made haste her bed to strew :

E'en to that bower, where first undone,
 Now yields its bed forlorn,
And now beholds a cherub son
 In grief and terror born.

" Ah, lovely babe !" she cried, " we part
 Ne'er, ne'er to meet again !"
Then frantic pierc'd its tender heart—
 The new-born life is slain.

Swift horror seiz'd her shudd'ring soul—
 " My God, behold my crime !
Let thy avenging thunders roll,
 And crush me in my prime!"

With blood-stain'd hands the bank beside
 Its shallow grave she tore.
" There rest in God," she wildly cried,
 " Where guilt can stab no more."

Then the red knife, with blood imbru'd
  Of innocence, she press'd ;
Its fatal point convulsive view'd,
  And sheath'd it in her breast.

* Beside her infant's lonely tomb
  Her mould'ring form is laid,
Where never flow'r is seen to bloom
  Beneath the deadly shade.

Where falls nor rain nor heavenly dew,
  Where sun-beam never shines,
Where steals along the fire so blue,
  And hov'ring spectre pines.

There, too, its blood-stain'd hand to wave,
  Her mournful ghost is seen,
Or dimly o'er her infant's grave,
  Three spans in length, to lean.

APPENDIX.

NOT having chosen to intermingle with this collection the very earliest productions of my childhood, I have merely subjoined them, leaving it to the option of those who have read the preceding ones, whether to peruse them or not; and simply thinking it necessary to state in their vindication, that they were written at the early ages of thirteen, fourteen, and fifteen.

SONNET.

WHERE the hoarse billows rush upon the shore,
  Where shrieks some screech-owl's melancholy voice,
Where the bleak winds in loud defiance roar,
  Where horror reigns—that spot shall be my choice.

Oh, Sleep! kind soother of the grief-worn breast;
  Oh, Health! bright jewel of the labouring hind;
Oh, Hope! dear cheerer of the mind distrest;
  Oh, precious blessings! where may I ye find?

Hope, soft sustainer, whither art thou fled?
  Oh, Laura! pour the balsam in my heart;
Then Sleep once more shall rest my aching head,
  And blushing Health her cheering sweets impart.

MEDITATION.

'TIS Meditation that delights to dwell
　　In deep seclusion ; silently to roam,
Oft list'ning thoughtful to the distant knell,
　　Which tolls some mortal to his narrow home.

Where rocks with sable brows o'erhang the main,
　　And foaming surges lave the slimy shore,
Where echo screams the lengthen'd sound again,
　　Where o'er the heath the winds unfetter'd roar.

Or oft, when eve her twilight stillness spreads,
　　She loves to wander in the lonely glade,
Where no rough wight, with feet unhallow'd, treads,
　　To break the chain by Meditation made.

Where yawns the precipice of depth unseen,

Where frowns some mountain's elevated brow,

Or where the moon shines o'er the haunted green,

From vulgar fear deserted long ago.

INVOCATION TO SLEEP.

OH, Sleep! kind god, approach thy gentle wand,
  And strew thy poppies round my aching head,
Lay on my lids thy soft, all-conq'ring hand,
  And pour thy brightest visions round my head.

'Tis thou alone canst hush in sweetest peace,
  Lull the loud sigh, and stay the starting tear,
In calmness bid each stormy passion cease,
  Close the sad lid, and still the anxious fear.

Then come, kind god, and chase my cares away,
  Sooth the poor flutterer of my beating breast,
With haggard Misery one moment stay,
  Nor fly, thus scornful, from a wretch distrest.

TO LAURA.

WHY frequent wanders in the dead of night,
   The pensive Laura thro' the forest's gloom?
Why dares, regardless, the terrific sprite?
   Why fearless paces by the dreary tomb?

Why, printless, does she leave her downy bed,
   For strange enjoyment thus alone to stray?
Now on a dewy sod recline her head,
   Now thoughtful gaze upon the moon's pale ray?

Where now has vanish'd the resistless smile?
   Where flown the sprightly mirth which tun'd her
      tongue?
Why now no more can joy the hours beguile?
   Why charms deep solitude a maid so young?

Say, is it melancholy sways thy mind?

Unconscious thou from whence proceeds **thy smart;**
But search thy bosom, **and an arrow find,**

For there the urchin, **Love, has left his dart.**

MADNESS.

OH, Madness! worst of ev'ry ill!
'Twere mercy more the wretch to kill,
   Than thou should'st give the blow :
Come racking grief, the frame destroy ;
Come agony, thy smart is joy,
   To Madness trifling woe.

Of Madness, see the tortur'd child,
First shedding tears, then laughing wild,
   And then convulsive groan:
Then comes Despair, with wide-stretch'd eye,
Tearing the soul with agony ;
   Or hear the harrowing moan.

See the damp cheek of pallid Dread,
Quick mantling, mount to furious red,
 Or glow with feverish pink :
Or see him shrink, and shivering sigh,
With quiv'ring lip and glassy eye,
 And then exhausted sink.

Deep Melancholy rules by fits,
Then gloomy Madness moping sits,
 Or straw, unmeaning, ties.
When oft, to shun the fancied lash,
From dizzying heights they fearless dash,
 And thus the victim dies.

MORNING.

SEE light the hills adorning,
  The lark begins her strains,
As brightly gleams the morning,
  Wide breaking o'er the plains.

See ev'ry star retiring,
  And ev'ry dew exhale,
See morn with joy inspiring
  The songsters of the vale.

Behold yon cloud, how glorious!
  That captive holds the sun,
Which now breaks forth victorious,
  His radiant course to run.

Begone, each little fairy,
   In misty robe array'd,
With ev'ry spirit airy
   That haunts the desert glade.

EVENING.

A DESCRIPTIVE PIECE.

NOW Sol, behind the mountain,
  Withdraws his golden rays,
That, lingering on yon fountain,
  Displays a liquid blaze.

With curious colours tainted,
  The slippery rocks are seen,
By Nature's soft hand painted,
  In azure, red, and green.

Yon mountain top, aspiring,
  To reach bright Heaven tries;
A purple tint acquiring
  From evening's vivid skies.

And now his toil suspending,
  The labourer quits the field;
And lo! the dews descending,
  Their sweetest fragrance yield.

The fleecy lambs reclining
  Supine on yonder steep;
His sportive care resigning,
  The shepherd wrapt in sleep.

Now to the sea extending,
  Sol throws his sinking rays,
While o'er the ocean bending,
  The drooping willow plays.

The glowing prospect fading
  As deepening dusk succeeds,
And darkness slow invading,
  It gradually recedes.

INDIFFERENCE.

INDIFFERENCE! nymph of calm, unruffled brow,
   I hail thee, henceforth, as a welcome guest;
Thy easy chain of flow'rets round me throw,
   And fix thy careless empire in my breast.

What! if unfelt by thee, transporting bliss,
   Unknown the raptures of love's thrilling smart;
Unfelt the eloquent, the tender kiss:
   Unknown, the melting movements of the heart.

And ah! unfelt the chastening rod of pain;
   Unfelt the thorns in love's seducing snare,
Unfelt the galling of a hopeless chain,
   Unknown the killing anguish of despair.

Ah, happy nymph! who would not be like thee,
  Insensible to Pleasure's dear extreme?
To be, too, from excess of anguish free,
  And glide thro' life on an unruffled stream?

WAR.

SEE bloody Discord lift her envious head,
   And shake the hissing serpents from her hair:
Then o'er the earth see wild Confusion spread,
   And hast'ning evils beckon to Despair.

Who now with cheerfulness shall smiling toil,
   And happy view the children of his care?
Say, who with industry shall dress the soil,
   For whom the wife her frugal store prepare?

Must the delight which deck'd the honest brow,
   The tender father sad and silent droop?
The smile contented, and the healthful glow,
   Alike be banish'd from the guiltless group?

Wild with despair, the mournful father flies
    To gain or death or glory in the field,
Distracted fights, to still his children's cries,
    And nobly bleeds, the bitter bread to yield.

The widow's tears must wet the harden'd ground,
    The scanty crust in tears his offspring steep;
Yet ceaseless still, no end those tears have found;
    For Father, Husband, Friend, they have to weep.

PEACE.

RETURN, sweet Peace, and shed thy glories round,
    And spread thy fair wings o'er a troubled isle;
No more let carnage stain the fruitful ground,
    And blood the works of Heaven's hand defile.

Shall Discord drive thee, mild-ey'd nymph, away?
    And Faction strike thee with its ruthless hand?
Shall Havoc mock thee on the crimson'd way,
    Confusion reign, and Ruin grinning stand?

Shall Famine point its all-consuming sword?
    And Misery reach the sunny cottage door?
Shall naught remain to deck the frugal board,
    Or bless the humble offspring of the poor?

Must the sad widow weep her loss in vain?
  The little orphan vainly ask for bread?
Yet still shall strife and sanction'd murder reign,
  And scalding tears be still unheeded shed?

TO LOVE.

AH! wherefore, cruel Cupid, didst thou bind,
　With such a painful wreath, my bleeding brows?
　Why give me only thorns? for ah! no rose,
No fadeless roses in my wreath I find.

When blinded by thy mother's guileful charms,
　Thou cam'st with Hope and Rapture in thy train,
　While close behind trod Woe and ambush'd Pain,
Lurking beneath false Pleasure's tempting arms.

Thy garland then with lively green was drest,
　And roses, which thou said'st would ne'er decay;
　And ah! we doubt not what our wishes say,
Till sad experience harrows up the breast.

Too soon, alas! that painful lot I found;
 For, withering in their bloom, the roses died,
 Shew'd the sharp thorns which they before did hide,
And time could never heal their treach'rous wound.

One only rose remain'd, and still look'd fair,
 Expiring Hope lay panting in its breast,
 I had no food to cheer the drooping guest,
Then, like the rest, it died, and left Despair.

TO LINDORF.

Oh! Lindorf! oh, Lindorf! for ever adieu!
  Thy heart beats no longer tumultuous for me,
Fair Laura has robb'd me of Heaven in you,
  And Laura alone must thy fav'rite be.

And canst thou so easy forget the fond breast
  That gave thee responsive a sigh for a sigh?
And canst thou despoil those sad eyes of their rest,
  That, when thine look'd tearful, disdain'd to be dry?

And canst thou repeat, without faltering tongue,
  Those oaths which to me thou hast plighted in vain?
Let Laura beware, for the snake which *has* stung,
  May the bosom which fosters it injure again.

Oh, Henry ! oh! why did I treat thee with scorn?
 Ah! why let thee scatter thy sighs to the wind?
Well art thou reveng'd ; 'tis now I that must mourn,
 For e'er having us'd thee, my Henry, unkind.

Dear hill! which, with him, I once lov'd to ascend,
 And view the red sun as it sunk in the west;
Dear lute! which did once thy sweet harmony lend,
 To charm and to sooth a fond lover to rest.

Bloom on, lovely rose-tree, in peace shalt thou blow,
 Thy buds evermore shall uninjur'd remain;
No roses do I want to deck my sad brow,
 A garland of thorns suits the temple of pain.

TO SYMPATHY.

SWEET Sympathy! thou fair, celestial maid,
   Thou precious, soft, indefinable tie,
   Source of the pitying drop that dims the eye,
Source of the sigh to Friendship's sorrows paid.

Divine inspirer! soul of the inmost soul!
   Bringing his mistress to the lover's sight,
   Though darkness pours around its deepest night,
And Ocean's wide expanse between them roll.

Oh, thou! descending on the downy wing
   Of Cupid, when he steals into the heart,
   Art mistress of the sweetly painful smart,
That, tipt with honey, bears a secret sting.

'Tis thou informest the fond lover's breast
  Of ev'ry sigh his absent Laura heaves,
  Of ev'ry tear its bright recess that leaves,
Bidding prophetic sorrow haunt his rest.

Oh! softer than the breeze to summer dear,
  Sweet as the breath of love, than snow more fair,
  Daughter of Heaven, and lighter than its air,
Thy robe a zephyr! and thy crown a tear!

TO OBLIVION.

OBLIVION, teach me, teach me thee to find;
 They tell me, in thy waters thou canst steep
Each sad remembrance of the troubled mind,
 And lull sharp Misery to eternal sleep.

And *canst* thou, goddess, in thy potent stream,
 Bid Retrospection yield its power to thine ?
 And Memory its sceptre too resign,
Making the past like a forgotten dream ?

Say, can thy magic stream procure repose
 To murd'rous Guilt, with restless, wide-stretch'd eye,
 Fearing Detection's torch for ever nigh,
And Justice with its scourge the scene to close?

Or canst thou bid Remorse withdraw its sting,
  Or cease to plunge its daggers in the heart?
  Lethean-like, erase the fest'ring smart
Reflection's bitter pangs ne'er fail to bring?

Say, canst thou lull upon thy Stygian breast
  The fiend Despair, than all the fiends more dire,
  With quiv'ring lips and eye-balls set in fire,
Canst thou so wild a demon sooth to rest?

Or shrieking Agony, with writhing brow,
  Convulsive sending forth the hollow groan?
  Or raving Lunacy, with harrowing moan,
Beseeching useless Pity for its woe?

If with thy power such miseries thou canst calm,
  Ah! let an hopeless wretch thy blessings prove,
Withhold not from his wounds the precious balm,
  That from remembrance blots unhappy love!

TO PRUDENCE.

HENCE, Prudence! bane of ev'ry virtuous deed,
　Child of cold Prejudice and selfish Fear,
　Insensible to Sorrow's bitter tear,
Wrung from the heart thou bid'st unpitied bleed!

Oh, Innocence! compell'd to seek the shade,
　And pine neglected in the cheerless wild,
　Defam'd by Slander, Envy's fav'rite child,
Weep on, for Prudence shuns thee, wretched maid!

Poor Honesty! bend not thy steps this way,
　Caution must scrutinize thy pale, wan face,
　On every guileless feature stamp disgrace,
And shuddering at thy guilt turn quick away.

Oh, Want! thou breathing image of cold death!
 By all forsaken, and by all forgot,
 And in a loathsome jail condemn'd to rot;
Avaunt thee!—for contagion taints thy breath.

Oh! Industry! made misery to endure,
 Steeping thy hard-earn'd crust in liquid woe;
 Contempt and Scorn shall heavier give the blow,
Thou must be indolent—for thou art poor.

If sad Experience e'er should steel my breast,
 Show me mankind, ungen'rous, cruel base,
 Ingratitude, the vice of all the race;
Then, Prudence! then I'll hail thee for my guest!

THE POWER OF LOVE.

THE sweet enthusiast, on a rock reclin'd,
  With transport listen'd to the dashing waves ;
Her snowy garments swam upon the wind,
  And Silence spread her wing amid the caves.

Now sportive Fancy did her eye-lids close,
  And Memory brought the happy past to view ;
A group of visionary friends arose,
  And in a dance confus'd around her drew.

Borne on Imagination's ardent wing,
  Again a child, she skimm'd the yellow mead,
Again threw pebbles in the cloud-pav'd spring—
  Again in baby gambols took the lead.

And now, her childhood past, a busier scene
   Floats on the bosom of the silent night ;
Her lover's form, all deck'd in sea-weeds green,
   Swam wet and shiv'ring in her startled sight.

Light on the trembling surge he seem'd to stand ;
   Pale was his face, loose hung his dripping hair,
His shroud he held within his clay-cold hand,
   And, sighing deeply, threw his bosom bare.

Then pointed Melancholy to the wave;
   " Say, wilt thou come, sweet love? behold my fate !
This element hath been thy lover's grave ;
   Say, dost thou love me still—or dost thou hate?"

In haste the beauteous dreamer op'd her eyes,
   To lose the vision from her rocky pillow ;
In vain, alas ! whatever side she tries,
   The sprite remains, still pointing to the billow !

And now a sterner look assum'd his face;
   " Thou dost not love me, or thou wouldst not stay,
Come plunge, my love !—soon, soon shall we embrace !
   Midnight has past :—haste, haste, I must away !"

The sweeet enthusiast heard her lover groan ;

And sighing from the promontory's steep,

" See, dear-lov'd spirit!—I am thine alone!"

She said ; and plunging sought him 'midst the deep.

EDMUND AND ANNA.

A LEGENDARY TALE.

NOW near drew the time when fair Ann was allow'd
   To visit her lover confin'd ;
To mingle her tears, as his sadly flow'd,
   And sooth the despair of his mind.

As she skimm'd o'er the wood, lo! the night-owl was
      heard
   To give three hollow shrieks from a tree ;
She stopt, listening, and thought the ill-omening bird
   Said, Thy lover has sorrow for thee.

Still onward she flew, while the envious wind,
　　Half jealous, retarded her pace;
Dishevell'd her garments to stay her behind,
　　Or furiously broke in her face.

Darkness reign'd on the earth, and from every spot
　　Horror seem'd unmolested to stare;
She trembled to pass her once favourite grot,
　　Lest Danger and Death should be there.

At length, like a lily new-wash'd in the dew,
　　She reach'd the drear prison's high gate,
And feebly she knock'd, while her fears stronger grew,
　　For her Edmund's unfortunate fate.

The long-dying echo she thought spoke his doom,
　　As the jailor pass'd slow through the hall,　[gloom,
The lamp beam'd from afar, pierc'd through the thick
　　And show'd the chill damps on the wall.

He open'd the gates, and along led the maid;
　　Dark sulkiness reign'd on his brow,
From his savage black eyes murd'rous guilt was betray'd,
　　And gall from each pore seem'd to flow.

The contrast how strong! he in sable array'd,
 Swift leading a virgin in white;
His form seen and lost 'mid the dubious shade,
 Like a fiend and an angel of light.

Anna scann'd o'er his savage appearance with dread,
 And shudd'ring, her eyes she withdrew;
The slimy walls shone in green, yellow, and red,
 As the lamp its weak rays on them threw.

Soon they reach'd a steep staircase form'd under the
 Poor Anna descended untold,   [ground;
For she knew the drear dungeon where Edmund lay
 A prey to want, famine, and cold.   [bound,

The keeper, nought heeding her love or her haste,
 Crept slow; and unlocking the door,
The dank vapours burst out which before were encas'd,
 And swam in a mist on the floor.

She enter'd, and heard the door bolted again!
 Edmund started, and flew to embrace;
Poor pris'ner, alas! the endeavour was vain,
 For his chain dragg'd him back to his place.

Now the damps they dispers'd, Anna saw on the stones
    Her lover distended and ill ;
A chain round his body contracted his bones,
    And prevented his breathing at will.

His hair hung disorder'd, his garments were loose,
    His wrists were encircled by chain ;
Yet all these oppressions could never induce
    Young Edmund's firm soul to complain.

" Ah ! wherefore, my Anna ! wherefore dost thou come
    To visit my dungeon so drear ?
Like morning's fair goddess dispersing night's gloom,
    The trav'ller far wand'ring to cheer ?

" Oh, Anna ! black midnight will speedily be,
    The poison ! the dagger ! are near,
So, farewell ! for ever farewell unto thee,
    Nay, start not ! what folly is fear !"

" Oh, Edmund ! I surely not heard thee aright,
    Or sorrow has injur'd thy brain !
What mean'st thou by dagger and poison at night ?
    Oh, Edmund ! my love, speak again !"

" I tell thee then, Ann, in the dead of the night,
   At the silent drear hour of one,
I shall be a memento of death in thy sight,
   A tenant prepar'd for the tomb."

" Oh, Edmund! my life! and oh, Edmund! my love!
   Is that then thy portion to be?
Thou shalt not go single, for I too will rove
   Through the fields of Elysium with thee."

" Forbear thee, rash beauty! say, what dost thou mean?
   Forbid it, thy Maker on high;
Thy time is not come to quit life's idle scene;
   Ah! wherefere should Anna then die?"

" No more, dear lov'd Edmund! I'll meet thee above,
   And rest with thee too in the grave;
E'en death shall not part me from him that I love;
   I'll die since I thee cannot save."

'Twas in vain for brave Edmund to kneel and to pray,
   Or beg for a while to be heard;
For Anna was reckless of all he could say,
   And steadily kept to her word.

" And art thou resolv'd then ? and canst thou forego
  The young joys that fly at thy nod ?"
" Yes, Edmund! I can, or wherefore say I so ?
  I love thee, but next to my God."

" Behold then this phial, there is that within
  Will quickly add one to the dead ;   [begin,
When the church clock strikes twelve 'twill be time to
  In an hour thy breath will have fled."

" I thank thee, dear Edmund! for now thou art kind,
  So farewell, my love, unto thee!"
" Ah! farewell, dear Anna! stay, stay thou behind,
  And die not, dear martyr, for me!"

He said, and embrac'd her ; loud rattled his chains,
  When the jailor appear'd at the door ;
His Anna rush'd from him ; transfix'd he remains ;
  Then sighing, sinks on the damp floor.

Once more through the wild woods she swift took her
  To the castle, and flew to her room ;   [way
There watch'd the slow minutes, and curs'd their delay,
  For retarding her sorrowful doom.

At length it struck twelve—she snatch'd up the dose,
  In agony shook it around,
And then to her pale lips applying it close,
  Drank it firmly to ev'ry ground.

In less than a minute the fumes caught her brain,
  Hot and heavily felt her head ;
Her eyes clos'd themselves, fire glow'd in each vein,
  And stagg'ring, she reel'd on the bed.

Her heart now it trembled, her pulse it beat slow,
  A deep sleep crept over each limb ;   [flow,
She spoke not, nor mov'd, scarce her blood seem'd to
  But never did death seem less grim.

Her maidens came in, and supposing she slept,
  Stood silently round and about ;
No visible marks the base poison had left,
  It ravag'd within, nor without.

Now sudden her face like an angel's appears,
  Irradiant beams shot around,
Bright stars seem'd descending in shoals from the spheres,
  And spangled with di'monds the ground.

Hark! hark! the church clock strikes the big hour of
    In that instant she opens her eyes !   [one!
Serenely then smiling, "Dear Edmund, I come,"
    She stretches her arms out, and dies !

THE END.

PRINTED BY D. N. SHURY, BERWICK STREET, SOHO